Raducanu's Fairy Tale in New York

Tony Harmsworth

2

Table of Contents

Copyright Page

ISBN: 9798836191665

Edited by Harmsworth,net
Copyright © Tony Harmsworth 2022

Cover photographs – tennis balls – © Shutterstock
Emma Raducanu – © 2021 Michelle V. Agins / New York Times / Redux / eyevine

Tony Harmsworth has asserted his moral rights.

Published by:
Harmsworth.net
Drumnadrochit
Inverness-shire
IV63 6XJ

Plan International

Plan International improves the life of girls in underdeveloped countries, improving health, hygiene facilities, education, preventing child marriage, and FGM[i]. Emma Raducanu has enjoyed amazing opportunities in life, millions of girls, particularly in the third world, do not.

To help improve the lot of other girls around the world, 20% of the author royalties earned by this publication, after editing, artwork, and production costs have been covered, will be donated monthly to Plan International U.K.

The Author

Tony Harmsworth is a fan, nothing more, nothing less. He watched Laver and the greats at Wimbledon in the sixties, the rise of Billie Jean King, Chris Evert, and Martina Navratilova over the next decades, including Virginia Wade's Wimbledon silver jubilee present for the Queen in 1977.

More recently, he has been a fan of Andy Murray, and watching Wimbledon in 2021, like many others, he was smitten by the joyful and exciting play of Emma Raducanu.

Normally, he writes science fiction, but on this occasion, he has decided to write about something even more far-fetched, even more ridiculous and totally unbelievable – *Raducanu's Fairy Tale in New York*.

INTRODUCTION

Note for non-British readers—Tony writes in British English, with U.K. spelling, punctuation, and grammar, but does use U.S. English words where appropriate.

Quotations from interviews, commentators, and pundits have been edited solely to remove typos, repeated words, tense changes, and stumbles. At no time has their meaning been changed. The origination of all quotations is cited in the endnotes.

I have not provided a ball-by-ball account of the matches but have given a rough idea of the length of each point, and often a description of how the point was won. This has been done to improve readability.

Thank you.

Tony Harmsworth, 26ᵗʰ June 2022

Emma Raducanu was born on 13ᵗʰ November 2002 in Canada to Ion Răducanu from Bucharest, Romania, and Renee Zhai from Shenyang, China.

When Emma was two years old, the family moved to the United Kingdom, and she holds both British and Canadian passports.

She began playing tennis at the age of five, but also experimented with many other sports, including karting; motocross, horse riding, skiing, basketball, golf, and ballet. A fan of Formula One, she is a self-confessed adrenalin junky, but also, the poor girl might have masochist tendencies as shown by her support of Tottenham Hotspur Football Club, of which I'm also a lifelong suffering fan. Her tennis idol is Simona Halep, and if she hadn't taken up the sport, she says she might have become a lawyer or entered finance.

At the age of thirteen, she was allowed entry to the International Tennis Federation and played in the Liverpool Nike Junior International event, which she won, becoming the youngest ever winner of an under-18 ITF tournament. She followed this with two further ITF titles in 2017, and went on to add further titles before turning professional in 2018.

That year, she also achieved the girls' quarterfinals of both the Wimbledon and U.S. Open. At the lawn tennis event, she defeated Leylah Fernandez who is featured later in this story.

During the Covid pandemic, she continued her studies, and in mid-2021, she obtained an A☆ in mathematics and an A in economics. These were suitable grades to apply for admission to top universities.

In July 2021, at the main Wimbledon Championships, she won her way through to the fourth round, becoming the youngest British woman to reach the last sixteen in the open era. She might have gone further but suffered breathing problems, prompting McEnroe to say it probably had all been a bit too much for her. It was taken out of context, and most seasoned professionals were amazed at her success shortly after passing her school examinations.

Her coach at Wimbledon was Nigel Sears, but he was replaced by Andrew Richardson for her first extensive trip abroad. Emma continued to pick up points during the U.S. tour, including those for becoming the finalist at the Chicago WTA125 tournament. Her Wimbledon result saw her seeded 31 as a qualifier for the U.S. Open. To enter the main draw in which she would compete as an unseeded player, she would have to win three qualifying games. At this point, Emma was ranked 150 in the world.

Emma is sponsored by Nike tennis clothing and uses a Wilson Steam 100 racquet painted as a Wilson Blade.

Eighteen-year-old, Emma Radacanu's Fairy Tale in New York was about to begin. The tennis world would be amazed.

1 Bibiane Schoofs—Qualifying Round One

It is important to note that when the number of rally strokes is mentioned, it is the total number for the point, not the player i.e., a serve and return of serve is two rally strokes.

Schoofs is a thirty-three-year-old professional player ranked 285 in the world who had a career high of 142. This made her roughly the same level as Emma, but with far more tournament experience. Certainly, no easy opponent for the still raw Raducanu.

In temperatures around 90 Fahrenheit (low thirties Celsius), the two women emerged into brilliant sunshine on court eleven at Flushing Meadows. Although there were many seats for spectators, with this being a qualifying match, there were very few present, except interested parties and the players' support teams. It was interesting to see that numbers watching her games during qualification gradually increased.

Emma walked onto court, carrying her large, crimson Wilson racquet bag. Her hair was in a roughly braided ponytail. She'd chosen to wear white tennis shoes, a red and blue 'slam' tank top, a vivid yellow sun visor and short, white, training shorts with blue piping. Rather a hotchpotch outfit compared with how she dressed in later rounds. Her opponent, from the Netherlands, wore a battleship blue top and dark blue fitted tennis skirt.

After warm-up on the navy-blue courts with green surrounds, Emma won the toss and served. All the U.S. Open courts now used automatic Hawkeye[ii], so there was just the umpire with ball-girls and boys on court. No line judges.

I should point out that the first match[iii] had no commentators, so I am unable to quote any expert opinions in the way I have during later rounds.

Schoofs won the first point of the game with a great shot landing on the line on the sixth rally stroke. Love fifteen.

Inauspiciously, Emma was then foot-faulted, the only time I have ever seen her do that, but she won the second point on the seventh stroke, making Schoofs hit into the net. Fifteen all.

That was followed by an ace wide in Schoofs forehand court. Thirty fifteen.

Another unreturnable serve for forty fifteen.

A six-stroke rally, which Schoofs hit wide. Game to Emma. One-love.

***

Schoofs' first service game. The fifth rally stroke was hit long by Schoofs. Love fifteen.

Good return, and Schoofs hit Emma's return long. Love thirty.

Emma's return finds the net. Fifteen thirty.

Another unforced error by Schoofs on the fifth rally stroke brings them to breakpoint.

Schoofs hits Emma's return into the net. Two-love.

***

Emma serves, and Schoofs hits the sixth rally stroke long. Fifteen love.

Unreturnable serve down the T. Thirty love.

Massive winner behind Schoofs on the third rally stroke. Forty love.

Good volley by Schoofs on the fourth rally stroke. Forty fifteen.

Good return from Schoofs and Emma hits into the net. Forty thirty.

Schoofs hits long on the sixth rally stroke as Emma was approaching the net. Three-love.

***

Schoofs serves. Good point down the line on the third rally stroke and Emma hits the net. Fifteen love.

Emma's return flies long. Thirty love.

Great return, Schoofs fires wide. Thirty fifteen.

Ace down the T. Forty fifteen.

Schoofs hits Emma's return into the net. Forty thirty.

Another serve down the T. Emma gets her racquet to it, but can't return. Game Schoofs. Three-one.

***

Schoofs' return flies long. Fifteen love.

Schoofs' fourth rally stroke shot goes long. Thirty love.

Schoofs' return long again. Forty love.

A longer rally. Schoofs tries to come into the net but volleys the ninth rally stroke long. Game to Emma. Four-one.

***

On the eighth rally stroke, Emma approaches the net and fires a backhand winner down the line. Love fifteen.

Emma returns into the net. Fifteen all.

The sixth rally stroke sees Emma hit Schoofs' forehand court corner. Fifteen thirty. Schoofs calls for a replay of the point. The ball hit the line by millimetres.

Almost identical point, Emma hitting the line from her backhand on the sixth rally stroke. Breakpoint for Emma.

Great return, and Schoofs hits into the net. Game Emma. Five-One.

***

Emma serving for the set. Schoofs' fourth rally stroke is hit into the net. Fifteen love.

Emma bamboozled the Dutch player who tried to come in on a poor approach shot. Emma felt the need to apologise when she smashed the eleventh stroke winner from beside the net with Schoofs unable to respond. Thirty love.

Schoofs could not return an excellent, deep second serve. Forty love.

A good return from Schoofs forces Emma to hit the third rally stroke into the net. Forty fifteen.

Schoofs can't return Emma's ninth rally stroke and the ball hits the net. Game and first set to Emma, six-one.

***

The temperature on court was still extremely high, and during the set break, Emma made use of an air-conditioning device provided by the tournament, blowing cold air over her face, neck, arms, and legs.

Emma won ninety percent of her first serves and seventy percent of her second serves in the first set. Could Schoofs improve during the second set?

Serving with new balls, Schoofs hits Emma's return into the net. Love fifteen.

Fifth rally stroke from Schoofs goes long. Love thirty.

Schoofs double faults. Love forty. Three breakpoints.

Emma returns into the net. Fifteen forty.

Emma's wild return is long and wide. Thirty forty.

On the sixth stroke of the rally, Emma overhits, and the ball flies long. Deuce. Three breakpoints saved by the Dutch woman.

On the sixth stroke, Emma runs in to smash a perfect volley onto the baseline. Fourth breakpoint.

Excellent serve and volley by Schoofs. Second deuce.

Emma hits the line on the sixth rally stroke. Breakpoint again.

Schoofs hits the eleventh rally stroke long. One-love.

***

Emma plays an amazing shot that hits the backhand court line on the seventh rally stroke. She jumps high into the air and crouches on her haunches in joyful satisfaction. Fifteen love.

Schoof's return goes long. Thirty love.

Schoof's return hits the net. Forty love.

Another overhit return of serve. Emma's game to love. Two games to love.

***

Schoofs serving. She comes into the net, but hits long on the fifth rally stroke. Love fifteen.

The fourteenth stroke of the rally sees Emma hit into the net. Fifteen all.

The eighth rally stroke has Emma hitting wide. Thirty fifteen.

Emma's return is too good and Schoofs hits into the net. She is now telling herself off about missed chances. Thirty all.

14

Emma's powerful shots make Schoofs hit the fifth rally stroke into the net. Breakpoint. Thirty forty.

Emma hits wide on the sixth rally stroke. Deuce.

Double fault. Breakpoint again.

Schoofs has Emma scampering back and forth and she hits the eighth rally stroke into the net. Deuce number two.

A winning crosscourt forehand return from Emma. Breakpoint.

Ace out wide. Deuce number three.

An eleven-stroke rally that Schoofs could have won, but hits wide, emitting a frustrated scream. Advantage Emma.

A much better game for Schoofs, but Emma's persistence and speed around the court was impressive. A good return saw Schoofs hit long. Three-love.

***

After the break, Emma's serving.

Schoofs hits long and wide on the fourth rally stroke. Fifteen love.

Great serve, and Schoofs' return flies long. Thirty love.

Same result. Forty love.

Third identical point gives Emma the game Four-love. Schoofs is becoming frustrated with herself and continually getting annoyed.

***

Schoofs serving.

Emma plays a forehand winner down the line on the eighth rally stroke. Love fifteen.

Emma's return is too good, and Schoofs hits the net. Love thirty.

A bit of good luck with the net cord turns sour as Schoofs manages to force Emma to hit into the net on the tenth stroke of the rally. Fifteen thirty.

Emma hits an outright crosscourt backhand return winner. Breakpoint. Fifteen forty.

Schoofs double faults to lose the game. Five-love.

***

Emma to serve.

On the eleventh stroke of the rally, Schoofs' shot hits the line and Emma mishits into the net. Love fifteen.

Emma's sliced shot after Schoofs' return spins wide. Is it nerves? Love thirty.

Ace out wide. Fifteen thirty.

Emma's approach to the net leaves her vulnerable to Schoofs' excellent lob. Fifteen forty. Finally, a smile on Schoofs' face.

Oh, dear. Emma appears over-confident, probably with some nerves trying to serve out the match. She hits an excellent serve, but her approach shot once more leaves her open to a lob. This time, her backhand overhead volley goes into the net. Schoofs has broken Emma's serve and avoided the bagel. Five-One.

***

Schoofs serving.

Emma hits the sixth stroke of the rally into the net. Fifteen love.

Schoofs hits the ninth stroke long. Fifteen all.

Emma hits into the net on the fourth stroke. Thirty fifteen.

Schoofs misses the opportunity to win a passing shot as Emma comes into the net. The ninth rally stroke goes long. Thirty all.

Emma returns poorly and Schoofs punishes her with a crosscourt shot that hits the line. Forty thirty.

On the sixth shot of the rally, Emma hits a winner behind Schoofs. Deuce.

A long rally sees Emma hit the fourteenth shot into the net. Advantage Schoofs.

Encouraged by breaking Emma's serve, Schoofs went on to hold her own service game after Emma hits long on the eighth stroke of the rally. Was Emma bottling the end of the match? It was now Five-two.

***

During the break, playing the air conditioning jet over her legs, arms, neck, and face, Emma looked pensive as she

16

prepared to attempt to serve for the match for a second time. More nerves ensued.

Excellent serve and a wild return. Fifteen love.

The fifteenth stroke of the rally sees Emma take the point. Thirty love.

Emma hits the fifth rally stroke wide, trying to do too much too soon with the point. Thirty fifteen.

Emma hits long on the fifth stroke, overhitting. Thirty all.

A great, unreturnable serve, and Emma screams, 'Come on!' as she reaches match point. Forty thirty.

Emma plays the rally steadily, not overhitting, not getting too close to the line, waiting for Schoofs to make a mistake. The tenth rally stroke flies long and wide from Schoofs' racquet. Game, set, and match, six-one; six-two. Emma was through the first qualifying round.

***

For those who like stats, 67% of Emma's first serves were in play and she won 81% of them. She also won 62% of her second serves; had two aces; no double faults; won five of twelve breakpoints in a match lasting one hour and one minute.

Next to come was a left-handed, twenty-three-year-old, Mariam Bolkvadze, the world number 167 from Georgia.

2 Mariam Bolkvadze—Qualifying Round Two

The Raducanu who walked onto court five for the second round of U.S. Open Qualifying, no longer looked like the kid in training shorts who beat, Schoofs, but was a beautiful young woman in Nike's NY Slam Outfit. It was the same tank top, but with a matching, glistening, blue tennis skirt with inset red pleats matching the top. This was a young, professional tennis player and looked every bit the determined teenager. Her outfit was crowned with the same yellow sun visor and white shoes.

Bolkvadze was dressed in a black tank top and tight tennis skirt with white shoes, the top of her right thigh heavily strapped. She won the toss and warm-up began. The temperature on court was a scorching 93 Fahrenheit (34 Celsius).

Commentator, Dave Leno[iv]: 'It's very hot conditions as we walked the grounds a few moments ago, so keep that in mind as it plays out.

'Raducanu is coming off a remarkable run in Chicago last week, where she reached the final.'

Jesse Levine: 'Look, I think a lot of people fell in love with her and she gained a lot of fans at Wimbledon. You know, she won a lot of matches there, and obviously playing in front of her home country like that in a Grand Slam, it's always nerve wracking and was impressive to watch her and boosted her confidence. And now she's very well known throughout the tour and not a newcomer anymore.

'I mean, now people are definitely taking eye on her and they're going to scout her a lot more. It's always different when you're coming fresh out on the tour and people don't know you and they don't know how your game is, what your strengths and weaknesses are. And then when you get that kind of exposure, everyone starts taking note and you know they start realising your tendencies where you go on the big points and know where you want to go, where you're

18

comfortable, where you're uncomfortable, so for her that's going to take a little bit of adjusting now that people really have taken notice.'

Dave Leno: 'Now, we're going to focus on this round two women's singles qualifying match. Raducanu lost the toss and will get us started on court five to the left of the chair.

'This can parallel also to your case, Jesse. Climbing from the juniors and on to the pro circuit, what's that pressure like for Raducanu, right now, at just eighteen years old, does well to slam in a major. I know you've been through that experience as well throughout your career.'

Jesse Levine: 'I think someone like Raducanu is definitely used to being in that spotlight, so for her that's nothing new. Obviously, playing junior tournaments and going to the pros is a little bit of transition, more of a physically demanding schedule. You're able to play a lot more tournaments and you know week after week you need that consistency.'

Emma to serve. Bolkvadze's return hits the net cord and although Emma got to it, she hit long. Love fifteen.

Bolkvadze hits the sixth rally stroke into the net. Fifteen all.

Bolkvadze hits the fourth rally stroke into the net this time. Thirty fifteen.

Emma hits the seventh rally stroke long. Thirty all.

Emma wins on the eleventh rally stroke. Forty thirty.

Dave Leno said, 'That's a good point there. Great job. Decided when the time was right, went behind her. Really smart tennis and good placement too, this one was right in the corner.'

Bolkvadze hits the fourth rally stroke long. Game to Emma. One-love.

***

The leftie comes out to serve. Emma overhits the sixth rally stroke. It goes a fraction long. Fifteen love.

Good return. Bolkvadze hits long. Fifteen all.

Emma's backhand return is rather wild and goes wide. Thirty fifteen.

Double fault. Thirty all.

Good ball strikes. Bolkvadze hits the net on the ninth rally stroke. Breakpoint. Thirty forty.

Great play. Emma just fails to pass Bolkvadze, but the Georgian could do no more than hit the net on the fifth rally stroke. Emma has the break. Two-love.

***

Emma serving.

Great one-two combination winning on the third rally stroke. Fifteen love.

On the sixth rally stroke, Bolkvadze plays a winner. Fifteen all.

Emma plays a great approach shot on the third rally stroke, but it turns into a winner on Bolkvadze's backhand side. Thirty fifteen.

Terrific net play from both women, but Bolkvadze passes Emma on the eighth rally stroke. Thirty all.

Bolkvadze plays the fourth rally stroke behind Emma, making her slip. Breakback point for Bolkvadze. Thirty forty.

Emma hits the seventh rally stroke long, going for a winner instead of extending the rally. That's the breakback. Two-one.

***

Bolkvadze serving. Emma's return flies long. Fifteen love.

Good return. Bolkvadze hits it wide. Fifteen all.

Excellent play from Emma has Bolkvadze scampering back and forth, then Emma hits behind her on the sixth rally stroke. Fifteen thirty.

Jesse Levine said, 'That's good stuff there from Raducanu. I like the way she recognises the short balls, really steps up into the court and she doesn't seem to mind finishing points at the net. She sees Bolkvadze coming up and making with the open racquet face, and just follows that in. She's very confident moving forward.'

Emma's backhand return just misses the line, probably aiming for too much, too soon. Thirty all.

She hits the fourth rally stroke into the net. Forty thirty.

Emma's return is a little short and Bolkvadze hits a winner to her backhand side. It's all square. Two games all.

***

Emma serves and Bolkvadze's return finds the net. Fifteen love.

Brilliant return of Emma's second serve. Fifteen all.

Bolkvadze hits the tenth rally stroke into the net. Thirty fifteen.

Emma hits the fifth rally stroke behind her opponent to win the point. Forty fifteen.

Bolkvadze hits the twelfth rally stroke into the net. Emma kept her ground strokes deep, waiting for the Georgian's mistake. Three-two.

***

During the break, both players sat with iced towels around their necks.

Bolkvadze to serve. Emma hits the fourth rally stroke into the net. Fifteen love.

Bolkvadze hits the seventh rally stroke wide. Fifteen all.

Then, Bolkvadze hits some deep shots into Emma's forehand side. On the eighth rally stroke, Emma retreats and Bolkvadze plays a winner into the same location. Thirty fifteen.

Double fault. Thirty all.

Bolkvadze mishits long. Thirty forty.

Dave Leno commented, 'She's got another breakpoint here, Jesse.'

'Yes,' Jesse Levine added, 'it's been a little bit of an up and down start to this set from Raducanu. She came out, started super solid, winning the first two games, and then had a little bit of a mental lapse there. Now, coming back into it and much more focused, far more solid after those third and fourth games.'

Emma mishits the eighth shot wide. Deuce.

Emma's return goes wide. Advantage Bolkvadze.

On the fifth rally stroke, Bolkvadze hits the net. Deuce.

Fifth rally stroke winner for Bolkvadze. Advantage.

Emma tries to do too much on the sixteenth rally stroke. Game to Bolkvadze. Three games all.

***

Emma to serve.

Bolkvadze hits the sixth rally stroke long. Fifteen love.

'Jesse, for those who already know you, what's the mindset of somebody going through qualifying and having to win three consecutive matches at this level?'

Jesse Levine: 'I mean, you just gotta take one match at a time, not look ahead of yourself and really take point by point. It's not easy. You're Raducanu here and you know you just came off such a big Wimbledon and now you're playing qualifying at another Grand Slam. You gotta take baby steps.

'I gotta tell you, Dave, she looks like she's really struggling right now with heat or something. She's definitely slowed down a little bit, Raducanu.'

Emma hits the eleventh rally stroke long. The long rallies don't seem to be helping. Fifteen all.

'I agree. I think the tempo has slowed down a bit on the Raducanu side, and as we mentioned, it's approaching 95 degrees at Flushing Meadows, New York.'

Bolkvadze's return wide. Thirty fifteen,

Emma hits Bolkvadze's return into the net. Thirty all.

Emma skies the seventh rally shot. She looks extremely tired. Thirty forty.

'Breakpoint here for Bolkvadze at 31 minutes. She has an opportunity to break Raducanu for the second time,' said Dave Leno.

Bolkvadze's fourth rally stroke is hit long. Deuce.

Emma shouts, 'Come on!' as Bolkvadze hits long on the seventh rally stroke. Advantage Raducanu.

Dave Leno: 'It's a big come back in this game. It's been a long game for Raducanu. She has a game point chance to remain on serve here towards the end of this first set on court five.'

22

Emma holds as the fourth rally stroke goes long. Four-three.

Dave Leno: 'That's perfect composure from the eighteen-year-old. Raducanu comes up with the hold after a shaky game there. Four to three in games.'

***

Throughout their break, Emma is keeping the air conditioning on her face and arms while taking on fluids and energy drinks. She's also sitting with an iced towel around her neck.

Bolkvadze serving with new balls.

Emma runs out to receive, apparently reinvigorated.

The seventh rally stroke from Bolkvadze hits the net. Love fifteen.

Bolkvadze hits Emma's return long. Love thirty.

Jesse Levine: 'Raducanu is doing a good job. Really making Bolkvadze play that extra ball right now. Not going for too much.'

Fifth rally stroke hit long by Bolkvadze. Love forty.

Emma's return hits the net. Fifteen forty.

Emma's fourth rally stroke goes long. Thirty forty.

Bolkvadze hits the fifth rally stroke into the net.

Dave Leno: 'There's the break for Raducanu! The second of this opening set.'

Five-three.

***

Emma is serving for the set.

Amazing return from Bolkvadze deep into Emma's forehand side. Love fifteen.

Emma races into the net to smash the seventh rally stroke beyond Bolkvadze's reach. She shouts out again. Fifteen all.

Emma serves deep into the lefty's backhand, then almost hits the line on the deuce side making Bolkvadze mishit into the net. Thirty fifteen.

On the eighth rally stroke, Bolkvadze hits a winner into Emma's forehand side. Thirty all.

Bolkvadze's return into the net. Emma screams out. Forty thirty. Set point.

Unreturnable serve, out wide. Game and first set to Emma. Six-three.

Dave Leno: 'Raducanu does it! She takes the opening set six to three with another fantastic serve out wide. Raducanu moves to the chair quickly and grabs the portable AC as well, yes, and deservedly so. Six-three and an opening set over Bolkvadze.

'Jesse, you and I commented a few times that we thought the tempo was going down. She was working hard and slower as the middle of the set was taking place, but when there was a four three score line at the changeover, it seemed like she refocused and yeah, she took that set.'

Jesse Levine: 'Yes, definitely. Conserve some energy and use it at the right time, but you can see her really trying to cool down with the ice towel and the portable AC unit. She's going to take her time here, but it was a really well managed first set there from Raducanu. Just a couple of loose games there but looking solid.'

***

During the break, Emma sat with an iced towel around her neck, also playing the air conditioning over her face and arms. She put a bag of ice under each thigh. Obviously feeling the heat. Bolkvadze disappeared for a bathroom break, returning with a bright yellow top. This gave Emma more time to cool herself down and prepare for the second set, so perhaps, not the best tactic from the Georgian. Emma chews on a banana.

Bolkvadze came out to serve, very determined.

Emma returns into the net. Fifteen love.

Emma can't reach and mishits the sixth rally stroke wide. Thirty love.

Bolkvadze hits Emma's return into the net. Thirty fifteen.

Thirteenth rally stroke hit into the net by Bolkvadze. Thirty all.

Jesse Levine: 'It's really good stuff there from Raducanu. Her shot selection has been pretty on throughout this match, so far, you know, making the right decisions especially here. She gets pushed back deep and goes back crosscourt instead of trying to go down the line. High percentage tennis. Her attitude has been great so far.'

Emma's return is too good and hit into the net. Thirty forty. Breakpoint for Emma.

On the seventh rally stroke, Bolkvadze plays a winner into Emma's forehand side. But she can't reach it. Deuce.

Emma's return hits the net. Advantage Bolkvadze.

Emma's return flies wide. Love-one.

***

Emma serving. The eleventh rally stroke sees Emma come into the net and play a forehand winner. Fifteen love.

Bolkvadze hits the fourth rally stroke wide. Thirty love.

Ace down the T. Forty love.

Good serve and came in to hit the winner off the return. Game to love for Emma. One game all.

***

The Georgian serving. Good winner for Bolkvadze on the fifth rally stroke. Fifteen love.

Thirteenth rally stroke is another winner from Bolkvadze. Thirty love.

Emma's mishit return flies long. Forty love.

Double fault. Forty fifteen.

Emma's return is in the net. Game to Bolkvadze. One-two.

***

With the ice towel around her neck, Emma rubs bags of ice over her thighs to cool down. She comes out onto the court to serve.

Bolkvadze's return flies wide. Fifteen love.

Five strokes in the rally, and Emma comes into the net on the third and volleys a winner on the fifth. Thirty Love.

Jesse Levine: 'I've been really impressed with the Raducanu net game throughout this match. She comes in on the right shots. The shot selection is there and with a volley

25

she does exactly what needs to be done—not too much but just enough to give her opponent that false hope that they're going to get there. It makes them run for it.'

Emma overhits the fifth rally stroke. Thirty fifteen.

Bolkvadze comes into the net on the fourth rally stroke, and Emma hits a great forehand passing shot. Forty fifteen.

Dave Leno: 'One of our best shots of the match right there on that pass. Big yell in jubilation there from Raducanu. Couple of game points.'

Bolkvadze's return goes long and wide. Two games all.

***

Bolkvadze to serve.

Good solid point for Emma. Love fifteen.

Emma's return very wide. Fifteen all.

Emma puts the sixth rally stroke into the net. Another unforced error. Thirty fifteen for the Georgian.

Emma hits an unforced error into the net on the sixteenth rally stroke. Struggling in the longer points. Emma hunches over and leans on her racquet after the point. Much more exhausted in the heat than the Georgian. Forty fifteen.

Another long shot on the sixth rally stroke gives Bolkvadze the game. Two-three.

***

Emma serves and hits Bolkvadze's return into the net. Love fifteen.

The return goes long. Fifteen all.

Bolkvadze skies the return, but rather than play a crosscourt volley winner, Emma plays down the line. The rally continues for two more strokes with Bolkvadze passing Emma who was still at the net. Emma looks slow and ponderous. Fifteen thirty.

Jesse Levine: 'Emma should have put away two of those shots.'

Big overhead smash on the ninth rally stroke brings out another yell from Emma. Thirty all.

Emma plays an unforced error into the net on the fifth stroke of the rally. Breakpoint.

26

Good return, and Emma, trying to play a winner, hits long. She looks tired. A worrying time for Emma. Another break. Two-four.

***

Dave Leno: 'We'll see how Raducanu comes out here, four two down.'

Bolkvadze serving and hits the seventh rally stroke into the net. Love fifteen.

Fifth stroke into the net by Bolkvadze. Love thirty.

Jesse Levine: 'Much more aggressive from Raducanu in this seventh game.'

Bolkvadze hits the seventh rally stroke into the net off Emma's passing shot. Love forty.

Dave Leno: 'Patience there from Raducanu. The opportunity right here, Jesse, to break right back.'

Bolkvadze hits Emma's return into the net. Game Emma.

Dave Leno: 'She earns the break! She storms right back, breaks for the third time in the match. The score's three, four. Back on serve.'

Three-four.

***

Dave Leno: 'Over 90 degrees out there in Flushing Meadows, New York. Hot, humid conditions.'

Emma serves and hits a winner off Bolkvadze's short return. Fifteen love.

Wide return from Bolkvadze. Thirty love.

Jesse Levine: 'Just get the feeling, ever since Raducanu went down a break in this set, she's kind of loosened up, started hitting her shots and freed up and really creating a lot more pace behind her shots now.'

Ace down the T. Forty love.

Another ace down the T. Another game to love. Four games all.

***

Bolkvadze serving.

Longest rally of the match. Emma waiting for Bolkvadze to make the error, which she does on the twenty-seventh rally stroke. A tiring point in the heat. Love fifteen.

Jesse Levine: 'They're both winded after that one.'

Double fault. Love thirty.

Emma's return goes long, and she shouts, 'Come on. *Come on!*' Fifteen thirty.

Bolkvadze comes in on Emma's return. Emma gets to the dropshot but can't win the next volley, which hits the net. Thirty all.

Bolkvadze hits Emma's return into the net. Breakpoint.

Emma hits the eighth rally stroke wide, off balance and probably trying to do too much to shorten the point. Deuce.

Bolkvadze wins the sixth rally stroke. Emma bends double and leans on her racquet again. Advantage to the Georgian.

Emma hits the eighth rally stroke wide while attempting a down the line winner. Game to Bolkvadze. Four-five.

***

Emma hugs her iced towel and air conditioning vent as she drinks water and a light pink drink too.

Emma starts with a double fault. Love fifteen.

A wild swing at Bolkvadze's return goes high and wide, giving Bolkvadze a chance, two points from a break for the set. Love thirty.

Bolkvadze puts the tenth rally stroke into the net. Fifteen thirty.

Emma pounces on a poor return and volleys a winner. Thirty all.

Another one-two combination, but this time with a forehand crosscourt winner. Forty thirty.

Bolkvadze puts the eighth rally stroke long. Game to Emma. Five games all.

***

Bolkvadze to serve.

Eleventh rally stroke sent long by Bolkvadze. Love fifteen.

Dave Leno: 'They're both really feeling the effects of the conditions. Approaching ninety-five degrees out there.'

Bolkvadze hits Emma's return into the net. Love thirty.

Double fault. Love forty.

Dave Leno: 'It's the fifth double of the match from Bolkvadze, the third in this second set. A couple of breakpoints for Raducanu to get it on her racquet too. One would think she would culminate this match in straight sets.'

Double fault again.

'Another double, the fourth in this set it and it ends up at a break for Raducanu, and she will be serving for the match and trying to get into the third round of qualifying.'

Six-five.

***

Emma uses the break to cool down, using ice bags, an iced towel, the portable air conditioning device and taking on energy drinks and sachets.

Emma returns to the court after the break to serve for the match.

Bolkvadze hits the tenth rally stroke into the net. Fifteen love.

Jesse Levine: 'I've been really impressed by the way she's come back in some of these games. We thought Raducanu might have been down and out, but she's really played smart tennis, conserved some energy as well, and really done a great job here at the end of the second set.'

Unreturnable serve. Thirty love.

Emma plays a winner on the fifteenth rally stroke. Forty love. Three match points.

Dave Leno: 'Excellent shot there by Raducanu. Terrific defending because those were two deep balls. She will have three match points. I'm really impressed.'

Jesse Levine: 'Raducanu's been closing out this match right now, especially serving for it, and you know, she's really showed no signs of nerves whatsoever. I thought about it in the middle of the second set, physically, she was starting to get a little tired. She definitely has her second wind right now.'

Emma runs in to Bolkvadze's return and plays the winner. Game set and match to Emma. Six three, seven five.

***

Dave Leno: 'Raducanu, the eighteen-year-old is through to the third round of qualifying at the U.S. Open. She wins in three and five over Bolkvadze on court five.'

Jesse Levine: 'That was impressive stuff from Raducanu today. Really showed why she is where she is right now, and as far as climbing up the rankings and backing up that result at Wimbledon, looked extremely impressive today. Really stayed solid. There were only moments when I felt she was physically getting a bit tired out there and had me a bit worried, but she pushed through and started playing smart. After she went down in that second set, she did a fantastic job of loosening up and started aiming for targets, becoming more aggressive again, and really, in that second set went straight back to what was working for her in the first set. Extremely impressive.'

Dave Leno: 'She broke Bolkvadze four times in the match at really key moments throughout this one, and had good composure, especially when it was a four three score-line in that opening set to take it six three, and then in the second set very late for Bolkvadze, the leftie. At times, it seemed like she was going to force a third set, but it wasn't to be.

'Yeah, I mean, you thought after Bolkvadze got that lead in the second set and, physically, she looked a lot stronger than Raducanu, but Raducanu really pushed through and dug deep and did a great job. So, really impressive stuff.'

Jesse Levine: 'Good to see her there getting back with her team after that win. They're going to be extremely happy, and you know, they can't be *too* excited and can be satisfied, as there is still one more match to go. One more match and she'll be in the main draw of the U.S. Open.'

Dave Leno: 'Looking to go there for the first time in her career after that round of sixteen advancement at Wimbledon.'

Stats: Emma had 73% first serves in play and won 73% of them. 56% second serves won with three aces and only one double fault. We weren't to know it at the time, but this was the hardest she had been pressed at any time in the tournament. No one was to get as close to taking a set from Emma as Bolkvadze.

Roll on the Egyptian, Mayar Sherif who stands five feet eleven, is twenty-five years old, and is number ninety-six in the world—a top hundred player.

3 Mayar Sherif—Qualifying Round Three

Once again, the action was to be on court five. We have the same commentators, Dave Leno and Jesse Levine, discussing important points[v]. Emma arrived in the same red and blue outfit she'd worn against Bolkvadze. Sherif wore a white sun visor, white tank top, and pink shorts.

Warm-up begins. In the qualifying draw, Emma is seeded number thirty-one with Sherif seeded four. Emma has a plaster just beneath her left knee. Cause unknown. Odd that we should see an injury in exactly that location at a critical time in the future.

Dave Leno: 'When you get to this point, Jesse, in qualifying with one step away from the main draw, it's going to be a tough test for Raducanu against Sherif, the number one Egyptian woman.'

Jesse Levine: 'Yeah. Sherif has been playing some really good tennis. She's a tough opponent and is very aggressive from the baseline, especially on her forehand side. She really likes to dictate points with the forehand. Raducanu, on the other hand, is coming off a really good week in Chicago, so she's playing really confident tennis, has two wins under her belt here in qualifying. We got to see her match the other day and she looked extremely solid out there. The heat was bothering her a little bit but also, she could have been tired from the past weekend, going far in the Chicago tournament, so let's see how she handles things today, and obviously nerves will come into play being one match away from qualifying for a major. So it will be interesting to see how both players handle their nerves today.'

Emma to serve.

Return out. Fifteen love.

Emma hits the seventh rally stroke wide. Fifteen all.

Sherif's return goes into the net. Thirty fifteen.

Same result. Forty fifteen.

Good passing shot off a short, high ball from Emma, on the eighth rally stroke from Sherif. Forty thirty.

Return goes long. A confident first service game for Emma. One-love.

***

The Egyptian to serve.

Emma has Sherif running from side to side until the Egyptian hits the eleventh rally stroke into the net. Love fifteen.

Double fault. Love thirty.

On the fifth rally stroke, Sherif plays a dropshot. Emma gets there and hits a backhand crosscourt volley passing shot. Three breakpoints. Love forty.

Emma's fourth rally stroke finds the net. Fifteen forty. Still breakpoint.

Sherif hits a passing shot winner after Emma returns poorly. Thirty forty. One breakpoint remaining.

Sherif hits the fifth rally stroke long. Emma has the break. Two-love.

***

Emma serves and hits the return from Sherif into the net. Love fifteen.

Emma volleys a skied return past Sherif. Fifteen all.

Sherif hits the eighth rally stroke wide, going for the line. Thirty fifteen.

Emma hits the ninth rally stroke hard and accurately. Sherif cannot get it back. Forty fifteen.

Great line touching backhand crosscourt shot on the fifth rally stroke, which Sherif gets to, but hits wide. Three-love.

***

Sherif serving.

A tremendous backhand winner for Emma on the fourth rally stroke. Love fifteen.

Dave Leno: 'A massive backhand by Raducanu, and that's been tailor made for her at the start of this match.'

Jesse Levine: 'Yeah, I mean, if she can step up and take the ball early like this on the backhand and place it like that, then she's in really good shape.'

Sherif hits Emma's return wide. Love thirty.

Dave Leno: 'You and I called the match with Raducanu and Bolkvadze. Must say that I think she's come out even stronger.'

Jesse Levine: 'Yeah, in this match, even though she won in straight sets over Bolkvadze. This is a huge start by her against Sherif.'

Ace. Fifteen thirty.

Sherif hits the fifth rally stroke long. Fifteen forty. Two breakpoints for Emma.

Emma hits the sixth rally stroke high and loopy. Sherif hits the reply long. Another confident break for Emma.

Four-love.

***

Emma serves.

Fifth rally stroke backhand down the line takes the point for Emma. Fifteen love.

Sherif returns into the net. Thirty love.

Then, Sherif hits the sixth rally stroke long. Forty love.

Next, Sherif's return goes long. Game to Emma. A win to love.

Dave Leno: 'It's a total domination of the first set. Raducanu is up five to love over Sherif in this set.'

Five games to love.

***

In the break, Emma chews on a banana and is using a bag of iced water on her thighs, cheek, and arms while sitting with an iced towel around her neck and the portable air-conditioning unit playing over her face.

Sherif serves. A huge return from Emma but it flies slightly long. Fifteen love.

This time, Emma's shot on the fourth rally stroke just misses the line. Perhaps, she's just overhitting to shorten the points in the searing heat. Thirty love.

34

A hard-hitting rally from both players. Sherif hits the seventeenth rally stroke high, and Emma passes her with a great smash. Thirty fifteen.

Dave Leno: 'I think those watching must be marvelling at the footwork and composure of Raducanu.'

Sherif comes in on the seventh rally stroke and plays a dropshot winner on the ninth. Forty fifteen. Can Sherif get on the scoreboard?

Emma returns into the net giving Sherif the hold and saving the bagel. Five-one.

***

Emma serves, and Sherif skies the return. Running right up to the net, Emma waits for it to land and smashes it into Sherif's forehand side. The Egyptian somehow manages to get her racquet to it, but the shot fails to clear the net. Fifteen love.

Jesse Levine: 'Both players serving well.'

Emma has 94% first serves in play.

Sherif hits the fifth rally stroke into the net. Thirty love.

Emma hits Sherif's return just long. Thirty fifteen.

This time, Emma hits the fifth rally stroke, a loopy ball from Sherif, long, perhaps going for too much, too soon. Thirty all.

Emma punishes a short return, and Sherif then hits into the net. Set point. Forty thirty.

With an unreturnable serve from Emma, she takes the set six-one in just twenty-four minutes.

***

Emma follows her same routine in the break, and they come out with Sherif to serve with new balls.

Sherif plays a great winner off Emma's return. Fifteen love.

Sherif wins on the seventeenth rally stroke. Thirty love.

Great wide return from Emma into Sherif's forehand, which finds the net. Thirty fifteen.

Sherif hits the fifth rally stroke long. Thirty all.

Emma's attempted forehand return flies wide and long. Forty thirty.

35

Emma gets Sherif to go wide and runs into the net with a great return and then passes her on the fourth rally stroke with a heavy backhand shot. Deuce.

Emma's shot on the fourth rally stroke flies long. Advantage Sherif.

Emma's backhand return is long. Game to Sherif. Love-one.

***

Emma to serve.

A great approach shot on the fifth rally stroke allows Emma's backhand to get the winner on the next shot. Fifteen love.

Sherif hits the sixth rally stroke wide. Thirty love.

Ace down the T. Forty love.

Sherif gets a great forehand passing shot on the fourth rally stroke. Forty fifteen.

Emma hits the third rally shot into Sherif's forehand corner. She gets it back, but Emma has come into the net and hits a forehand smash winner behind the Egyptian. Game to Emma. One game all.

***

Sherif serving, hits Emma's return long. Love fifteen.

Emma returns into the net. Fifteen all.

Sherif hits the fifth rally stroke beyond the baseline. Fifteen thirty.

Big kick-serve from Sherif and the return goes high and wide. Thirty all.

Sherif hits Emma's return into the net. Breakpoint. Thirty forty.

Sherif's slice on the fifth rally stroke makes Emma hit into the net. Deuce.

Next, Sherif hits the fifth rally stroke into the net. Second breakpoint to Emma.

Sherif moves away from the T for this serve and forces Emma wide. She returns fine, but Sherif's next shot lands right on the line and Emma can't reach it. Deuce two.

Big backhand crosscourt winner from Sherif on the fifth point of the rally. Her advantage.

36

Emma hits the fourth rally stroke long and wide. Huge shout from Sherif as she wins the game. One-two.

***

Emma serving.

Sherif wins on the seventh rally stroke. Love fifteen.

Emma hits a one-two winner off Sherif's return. Fifteen all.

Sherif hits the sixth rally stroke long. Thirty fifteen.

Good deep shots from Sherif, and Emma hits the ninth rally stroke long. Thirty all.

Emma's serve is unreturnable. She shouts out as the return hits the net. Forty thirty.

Sherif's return goes way long. Game to Emma. Two games all.

***

The Egyptian woman serves. Great return, and Sherif hits into the net. Love fifteen.

Sherif's shot on the ninth rally stroke goes long. Love thirty.

Emma comes into the net after her deep return and plays a neat forehand volley dropshot to win the point. Breakpoint. Love forty.

Emma gets the break on the fourth rally stroke—breaking to love. Three-two.

***

Emma, serving, plays the ninth rally stroke into the net. Love fifteen.

Double fault. Her first double. Love thirty.

Sherif's sixth rally stroke goes long and wide. Fifteen thirty.

Emma plays a backhand crosscourt winner on the ninth rally stroke. Thirty all.

Another double fault gives breakpoint to Sherif. Thirty forty.

Sherif's return goes high and lands on the corner line. Emma hits back at her as she approaches the net. There's a short sequence of volleys until Emma's shot on the ninth

37

stroke hits the top of the tape and bounces wide. Sherif has broken back. All square. Three games all.

***

Sherif serving.

Good, steady ground strokes from Emma, waiting for Sherif to make an error, which she does on the thirteenth rally stroke, hitting wide. Love fifteen.

Sherif hits a series of shots into Emma's backhand then on the seventh rally stroke hits a winner onto the line. Fifteen all.

Sherif hits the seventh rally stroke long. Fifteen thirty.

Sherif shuffles along the baseline and serves very wide, hitting Emma's scrambled return wide into Emma's forehand side, which Sherif didn't expect her to get to, but she does, and the rally continues until the eighth rally stroke when Emma hits the winner. Two breakpoints.

Emma overhits the return. Thirty forty.

Emma hits a backhand crosscourt winner on the tenth rally stroke to break the Egyptian's serve. Game Emma. Four-three.

***

Emma to serve.

Emma hits Sherif's return long. Love fifteen.

Sherif hits the fourth rally stroke long. Fifteen all.

The fifth rally stroke is hit very deep by Emma, and Sherif hits it into the net. Thirty fifteen.

Sherif's return is in the net. Forty fifteen.

Emma pounces on Sherif's return and plays a winner across the court. Five-three.

***

Serving, Sherif has Emma scampering and the fourth rally stroke goes into the net. Fifteen love.

Dave Leno: 'What stands out about Raducanu playing through the qualifying rounds?'

Jesse Levine: 'I'd think, right now in this match, it's her ability to take time away from Sherif. She's not letting Sherif breathe throughout this whole match. There was the little lapse in the one game where she got broken back after going up a break earlier in the second set. But she's really stayed on game plan and doing a great job of taking the ball early, especially the backhand crosscourt or backhand down the line. It's been incredible.'

Sherif hits the ninth rally stroke into the net. Fifteen all.

Good shot for Sherif off Emma's return. Thirty fifteen.

Sherif just misses a crosscourt shot. Thirty all.

Sherif scrambles to play a winner down the line.

Dave Leno: 'It's big from Sherif.'

Jesse Levine: 'It's a really tough shot. Did that perfect.'

Dave Leno: 'Look at that angle [on the replay]. That's a really tough shot Sherif made look easy at a big game point.'

Forty thirty.

Sherif puts Emma's return into the net. Deuce.

An unforced error by Sherif gives advantage to Emma. Match point.

Emma hits the eighth rally stroke high and wide. Deuce again.

The tenth rally stroke is missed by Sherif after a great running shot by Emma. Match point number two. Advantage Emma.

Sherif hits a winner off a tentative return. Third deuce.

Emma hits the eighth rally stroke a fraction wide. Game point for Sherif.

Emma hits the fourth rally stroke into the net, putting the pressure on herself to serve for the match. Game for Sherif. Five-four.

***

Emma serving for the match and to participate in the main draw.

Dave Leno: 'Second serve. What a response there. That second serve out wide. Fifteen love.'

Jesse Levine: 'That's how you start out a game serving for the match—second serve, ace!'

The return hits the net. Thirty love.

Another return into the net. Forty love. Three match points.

A fantastic wide ace!

Dave Leno: 'And for the first time in her career, eighteen year old Raducanu is into the U.S. Open main draw. She went one and four over Mayar Sherif and her career blossoms here in the United States.'

Jesse Levine: 'Raducanu looked solid throughout that match today. Did a great job of really taking the ball early and not letting Sherif get settled at any point in the match. She served extremely well throughout the match, did a great job and she can be excited to be through to the main draw. She can enjoy it today. What a moment for Raducanu!'

Match won, six-one, six-four.

***

Stats were 79% first serves in and 78% won. 50% second serves won with three aces and two double faults.

As Emma walked off the court she screamed, 'Yes!' over to her team.

4 Stefanie Vögele—U.S. Open Round One

Emma spoke to Mark Petchey[vi] about her upcoming main draw match. He congratulated her on qualifying and told her that so much had changed in her life, but the one thing that hadn't changed was that she kept winning.

Emma: 'I feel as though nothing has changed on my end because after Wimbledon it was straight back to training, and then I came out to the states to compete, and afterwards it was just focusing on the next match, so I'm just really enjoying my time on the tour. It's my first road trip and I can't wait to see how far I can go this week.'

Petchey asked whether it surprised her how quickly she had been able to win matches on the WTA[vii] tour and Wimbledon.

'Yeah, it has surprised me, because I was just thinking of a schedule before Wimbledon and was planning some 125 [point] events in Europe. Now, my schedule is completely changed and I'm here. Even now, playing WTA events is just really cool. To be able to play these top girls week in week out, I think that's the reason I play tennis, just to be able to test myself against the best in the World.'

He asked if she knew anything about her next opponent, Stephanie Vögele.

'No, I don't know much about her, but we'll see later on, I know she played Jodie Burrage in qualifying, and it was a tight match. I'm sure every single player here in the qualies or main draw is a great player. The margins are very small so she will be a tough match, but I'm feeling good about my game and feel confident.'

When asked if she had researched Vögele, Emma said, 'I spend a bit of time on all my opponents. I like to know what's gonna come up,' and she broke into her winning smile.

It is important at this point in the story to note that apart from some junior titles and the three wins in early rounds at

41

Wimbledon, Emma had not achieved a great deal. At an earlier age, Tracy Austin had won majors and was already a force to be reckoned with. I mention this here, as the following comments on her game by tennis pundits speaking on Amazon Prime before the first round of the U.S. Open genuinely show they were aware that Emma was someone particularly special. It is also important to note that Tracy Austin had been playing the tour for a good while before her teenage successes.

Catherine Whitaker[viii] said to Daniela Hantuchova, 'She does seem to have it all, doesn't she? It is very difficult not to get carried away about Emma Raducanu. We want to sort of limit the pressure that we heap upon her, but Danny, she does seem to have all the tools!'

Daniela Hantuchova: 'Absolutely, yes, and on top of all that, she's just such a joy to watch. You can't help but smile when you see her on the tennis court because how much she's enjoying it, and it's so nice to see someone being new to the process, new to the tour. Everything she does, everywhere she goes, is all the places that she ever dreamt of. Now, she's part of it so it just brings even more energy to her to work harder. As we know, she is a very disciplined girl, and puts so many hours on the court. I mean, to me, she is already one of the fittest players we have, and the way she's balanced on her shots, wonderful ground strokes and nothing much can go really wrong as it's very simple, it's very compact. I think that's where Nigel[ix] [Sears] did such a good job, just shortening it up, making it simpler. That's what we see, that potential. I think, you know, we are experiencing something special and I'm a huge fan of Emma.'

Annabel Croft: 'It's such an exciting moment for her, isn't it, because she has earned the place here by those three very tough matches and she didn't drop a set. Also, it's tough to get through qualifying but she's done it, so she's earned her position. I think it's also incredibly impressive, having reached the fourth round of Wimbledon, it's a great big announcement on the big stage and has woken up the rest of the tour, and you have some momentum going.

'It's very big, underlying her strength of character, to have been able to do that. Not only did she reach that final recently on a small level event, then come through qualifying so she will be in a really good place. That toughens you up. I think she has a great chance to get through this, and who knows what else she can do because I think, as Daniela said, she's got it all. Compact swings, great techniques, nothing can go wrong and a great athlete, so she is a story to watch.'

Tim Henman, talking courtside during warmup: 'Andrew [Richardson, her new coach] has history with her. They've known each other for a long time and Andrew obviously knows the family as well, which I think is important. [Andrew coached her aged eleven and twelve]. When you look at her game, whether that's technical or physical, there don't need to be many changes. She has fantastic technique, she is a great athlete, so I think continuity is important and just making sure she's aware of her opponents and some of their strengths and weaknesses. It's going to be interesting to see how this partnership evolves as it hasn't been going for long at this level but it's certainly moving in the right direction.'

They're out on court seventeen. Emma dressed in her red and blue slam outfit with white shoes, yellow sun visor and pearl earrings. Vögele, aged 31, in a pale blue top, visor and shoes with a pleated, dark blue skirt, her blonde hair in a loose ponytail.

Emma to serve first and she hits the fifth rally stroke into the net. Love fifteen.

Vögele returns into the net. Fifteen all.

Vögele's return long. Thirty fifteen.

Her opponent's fourth rally stroke is also long. Forty fifteen.

Emma wins the game on the ninth rally stroke. One-love.

***

Vögele serving, hits the thirteenth rally stroke long. Love fifteen.

Emma's return hits the net. Fifteen all.

Emma hits the sixth rally stroke wide. Thirty fifteen.

Great forehand from Emma on the eighth rally stroke. Thirty all.

Emma's backhand crosscourt shot goes into the net on the eighth rally stroke. Forty thirty.

Terrific backhand crosscourt return causes Vögele to hit into the net. Deuce.

Emma's return goes wide. Advantage Vögele.

Poor return and Vögele capitalises, hitting the third rally stroke into Emma's empty forehand side. Game Vögele. Emma manages to lose the game rather than Vögele winning it. One game all.

***

Emma serves again and Vögele's return goes long. Fifteen love.

Double fault. Fifteen all.

Emma hits Vögele's return into the net. Fifteen thirty.

Emma hits the fifth rally stroke very wide. Breakpoint. Fifteen forty.

Vögele comes in on the thirteenth rally stroke and plays a simple winner into Emma's forehand side to get the break of serve. One-two.

***

Vögele serving. Emma hits the fourth rally stroke onto the line. Love fifteen.

Vögele hits Emma's return into the net. Love thirty.

This time, Vögele sends the ball long off Emma's return. Love forty.

Emma gets a breakback to love when Vögele hits Emma's return long again. Two games all.

***

Emma serves and the return is hit into the net. Fifteen love.

Vögele hits the fourth rally stroke long. Thirty love.

Great one-two from Emma. Forty love.

Vögele hits long, giving Emma a game to love. That's eight points in a row. Three-two.

***

Good serve by Vögele. Return finds the net. Fifteen love.

Vögele hits the fifth rally stroke into the net. Fifteen all.

Longer rally. Vögele hits the fifteenth rally stroke wide. Fifteen thirty.

Vögele puts Emma's return into the net. Fifteen forty. Two breakpoints.

Emma hits the eighth rally stroke into Vögele's forehand side from the backhand, winning the game. Four-two.

Commentator, Sam Smith: 'Emma has the measure of it. Three games in a row for the eighteen-year-old. Anne, what a response to being broken in the third game.'

Anne Keothavong: 'She's settled out here and she is starting to let rip. Better court position as well from the Brit, further up the court ready to take it on.'

***

Emma serving.

Great shot from Vögele on the fourth rally stroke, finds the line. Love fifteen.

Vögele's return bounces before the net. Fifteen all.

Emma hits a backhand winner down the line off Vögele's return. Thirty fifteen.

Ace down the T. Forty fifteen.

Emma hits long on the fifth rally stroke. Forty thirty.

Vögele hits the fourth rally stroke into the net. Game to Emma. Five-two.

***

New balls, Vögele serving to save the set.

Emma hits the fourth rally stroke into the net. Fifteen love.

Double fault. Fifteen all.

A fabulous forehand crosscourt winner from Emma on the fourth rally point. Fifteen thirty.

45

A similar shot on the eighth rally stroke, but this time down the line, brings up another two breakpoints and two set points. Fifteen forty.

Sam Smith: 'It hasn't taken her long has it to find her feet in this match up against the far more experienced opponent. Raducanu, on her debut here, has really quickly arrived at two set points.'

A stunning forehand crosscourt winner sees off the first set.

Anne Keothavong: 'That's it by six games to two. What a performance. What an opener from the youngster!'

Six-two.

***

Winning the game on a break, Emma comes out in the second set to serve first.

Vögele returns into the net. Fifteen love.

Unreturnable serve. Thirty love.

Vögele returns into the net again. Forty love.

Emma puts the fifth rally stroke long. Forty fifteen.

Another unreturnable serve. Game to Emma. Six in a row. One-love.

***

Vögele serving.

Emma puts the eighth rally stroke long. Fifteen love.

Emma's return flies wide off a good serve. Thirty love.

Unreturnable serve from Vögele. Forty love.

Emma hits the fourth rally stroke for a forehand winner. Forty fifteen.

Emma puts the fourth rally stroke into the net. And Vögele stops the run of six games against her from increasing. One game all.

***

Emma to serve. She can't reach Vögele's shot on the eighth rally stroke, and it skids off her racquet. Love fifteen.

Vögele throws her racquet at Emma's seventh rally stroke and gets a great forehand crosscourt winner. Love thirty.

46

Great down the line return. Love forty. Three breakpoints.

Emma's seventh rally stroke drifts left. Love break game to Vögele. One-two.

Anne Keothavong: 'Given what happened in the first set, I don't think it's a good idea to break Emma—you get quite a severe response.'

***

Vögele serves. Emma plays a wonderful forehand crosscourt winner return. Love fifteen.

Emma's powerful return is hit into the net by Vögele. Love thirty.

Tenth rally stroke forehand crosscourt winner for Emma. Love forty. Three breakback points.

Vögele plays a down the line winner off Emma's return. Fifteen forty.

Vögele hits Emma's return long. Two games all.

***

Emma to serve.

Fifth rally stroke backhand crosscourt winner for Emma. Fifteen love.

Seventh rally stroke forehand down the line winner for Emma. Thirty love.

Emma hits long off Vögele's return. Thirty fifteen.

Emma's smash on the fifth rally stroke leaves Vögele stranded. Forty fifteen.

Vögele's return flies long. Game to Emma. Three-two.

***

Vögele serving again. The games are flying by.

Backhand down the line from Vögele, off Emma's return. Fifteen love.

Emma's return missed by millimetres. Thirty love.

Ace down the T. Forty love for Vögele.

Backhand crosscourt winner from Emma on the fourth rally stroke. Forty fifteen.

Vögele hits the seventh rally stroke long. Forty thirty.

Fifth rally stroke long from Vögele. Deuce.

Ace down the T. Advantage Vögele.

Vögele puts Emma's return into the net. Deuce.

Vögele hits the seventh rally stroke long. Breakpoint.

Emma plays wide on the eighth rally stroke. Deuce number three.

Emma places the fourth rally stroke into the net. Advantage Vögele.

A long rally, and on the fourteenth rally stroke, Emma hits a great backhand crosscourt winner into the corner of the court. Fourth deuce.

Emma's return hits the net. Advantage Vögele.

Emma's return long. Game Vögele. Three games all.

***

Emma to serve.

Fifth rally stroke winner from Emma with a backhand down the line. Fifteen love.

Vögele hits the sixth rally stroke wide. Thirty love.

Superb return from Vögele off a second serve. Thirty fifteen.

Return flies long. Forty fifteen.

Return into the net. Game to Emma. Four-three.

***

The Swiss player to serve.

Emma forces Vögele to hit the sixth rally stroke wide. Love fifteen.

Vögele hits the thirteenth rally stroke into the net. Emma looks as if she is just in hitting practice. Love thirty.

Emma hits the fourth rally stroke wide. Fifteen thirty.

This time, the same rally stroke goes long. Thirty all.

Long rally. Vögele hits the fifteenth rally stroke long. Breakpoint. Thirty forty.

Good serve by the Swiss player allows her to play a crosscourt winner off Emma's return. Deuce.

Emma returns into the net. Advantage Vögele.

Vögele puts the tenth rally stroke into the net. Deuce.

This time, it's the twelfth rally stroke into the net. Advantage Emma.

Emma plays a crosscourt forehand winner into the corner of the court. Five-three.

48

***

Emma serving for the match.

Vögele plays a winner on the twelfth rally stroke. She is not going down without a fight. Love fifteen.

Emma has Vögele running back and forth along the service line, then approaches the net and hits the seventh rally stroke, a forehand volley into the open space. Fifteen all.

Wide ace. Thirty fifteen.

Vögele hits the fourth rally stroke into the net. Match point. Forty fifteen.

Sam Smith says, 'A performance beyond her years. Raducanu with match points.'

Emma immediately double faults to forty thirty. There must be some nerves after all.

Sam Smith: 'That's okay. She's not done this before—not here, anyway.'

Then, a rather tentative shot is fired back. A winner by Vögele on the eighth rally stroke to bring up deuce.

Emma screams out, 'Come on!' as Vögele hits her next return into the net. Match point again.

Emma serves, Vögele returns and Emma's unforced error goes into the net. Second deuce.

Sam Smith: 'Getting nervous, Annie? You've gone very quiet beside me.'

Emma hits the fifth rally stroke into the net. Advantage Vögele.

Emma manages to pull off a delightful crosscourt semi-dropshot, which lands on the line on the fifth rally stroke. Third deuce.

Anne Keothavong: 'I didn't know she had one of those in her locker. She's kept it very quiet.'

Vögele hits the return into the net for advantage to Emma, who screams 'Yes' at the crowd in general.

Emma hits the fifth rally stroke wide as she attempts a backhand crosscourt shot. The fourth deuce.

Vögele hits the fourth rally stroke long to bring up a fifth match point.

Emma hits a lob on the eleventh rally stroke, and it lands long. Deuce again. Number five.

A timely second ace down the T brings up a sixth match point.

Emma double faults again! Deuce six.

A fantastic overhead backhand volley creates the seventh match point on the seventh rally stroke.

Sam Smith: 'I don't think even she thought she could pull that off.'

Anne Keothavong: 'I've got the feeling that she's not played too many of those before.'

Sam Smith: 'Ten minutes in this game.'

The Swiss player hits the sixth rally stroke into the net and a beaming, smiling, laughing Emma Raducanu has won her first-round match at the U.S. Open. Six-two, six-three.

***

Stats—77% first serves in play, 66% won, and 46% second serves won. She also won 76% of the points against Vögele's first serve and hit twenty-four winners.

After the match, Karthi Gnanasegaram interviewed Emma.

Karthi Gnanasegaram: 'Congratulations, Emma. You're into the second round on your debut at the U.S. Open. The crowd are clearly wanting to take selfies with you. This is a victory you can enjoy, isn't it?'

Emma: 'Yeah, it's actually incredibly amazing. I think everyone could tell that I was a bit shaky in the last game, I think I had five or six match points, but I got there eventually, I was just so relieved at the end of it. The crowd helped me so much and it feels amazing to be playing in front of fans again and over here in the States. They made me feel so welcome and so at home, so I really, really appreciated that. I feel really good physically and really confident in my game, so I'm just excited to see how far I can go.'

Karthi Gnanasegaram: 'You've come through three rounds of qualifying in brutal heat, during those games, and now in this one, you haven't dropped a set yet. How pleased are you with your performance? When you get broken you come straight back.'

'Yeah, I'm extremely pleased. I got broken early in both sets but managed to get a few returns, very clean out the middle of the frame, sort of by luck, sort of by skill, so I'll take it and run with it and use it to my advantage in the end.'

'We'll see you in the second round against Shuai Zhang.'

5 Shuai Zhang—U.S. Open Round Two

Zhang is a professional tennis player, born in Tianjin, China. She stands five feet ten inches tall, and at the time of this match, was thirty-two years old. She has been a quarterfinalist in both the Australian and Wimbledon Grand Slams, and she has also been a Grand Slam doubles champion in Australia. She's won two singles titles—Lyon in 2017, and Guangzhou in 2013. At the time of this match, Zhang is forty-nine in the world, so a considerably higher ranked and more experienced player.

Emma had played Zhang just three weeks earlier at the San Jose Silicon Valley Classic where she lost three-six, two-six in the first round.

Anne Keothavong[x]: 'Today will be a tougher challenge for her [Emma] though, as Zhang, who she played just four weeks ago in San Jose, admittedly that was Emma's first match post Wimbledon and she was looking a little rusty, but she didn't serve particularly well that day. She barely won any points behind her second serve. Her forehand was off but she's looking a lot sharper now she's had a lot more matches under her belt and the conditions here seem to suit her.'

Greg Rusedski: 'I watched that match as well. Her second serve was punished. Zhang was stepping inside the baseline, attacking, going quick and to the forehand side, willing to come forward, so she is going to put Raducanu off balance. Is she going to learn how to deal with this, as she and Andrew Richardson need to sit down and understand what happened in San Jose? In my opinion, she is the slight underdog in this match, even though we're expecting her to come through.'

They are out on court ten for this second-round match. Emma in her familiar red and blue slam outfit, and Zhang in an indigo two-piece tennis outfit with white baseball cap and shoes. Zhang won the toss and chose to serve.

First point, an unforced error by Zhang on Emma's return. Love fifteen.

Emma ran in on the ninth rally stroke from Zhang and hit an outright crosscourt forehand winner. Love thirty.

Annabel Croft: 'I think already it's a very different start, isn't it? Raducanu out of the blocks quickly, which she wasn't in the previous match.'

Double fault. Love forty.

Zhang hits Emma's return into the net. A break to love. Emma is up and running. One-love.

***

Emma serves.

Zhang's return catches the top of the net and rolls over. Love fifteen.

Emma hits Zhang's return into the net. Love thirty.

Zhang hits the sixth rally stroke wide. Fifteen thirty.

Emma is well inside the court to hit the fifth rally stroke and it sets her up for a winning volley at the net. Thirty all.

Zhang mishits the return of serve and it skies the ball out of the court. Forty thirty.

Zhang hits the fourth rally stroke long. Game to Emma. Two-love.

***

Zhang serving.

Emma hits the eighth rally stroke into the net. Fifteen love.

Zhang comes into the net and volleys a winner on the ninth rally stroke. Thirty love.

Good ground strokes from Emma, and Zhang hits the eleventh rally stroke long. Thirty fifteen.

Emma hits the fourth rally stroke into the net and jumps up and down in frustration at the error. Forty fifteen.

Great second serve from Zhang, very deep and wide. Emma's racquet just manages to deflect it, but no more. Good hold by Zhang. Two-one.

***

Emma serves and the return is skied wide. Fifteen love.

53

Sam Smith: 'Really nice service motion, has great composure setting up for the serve every single time, takes her time, very nice straight ball toss.'

Zhang's return goes long. Thirty love.

This time, Zhang hits the fourth rally stroke long. Forty love.

Annabel Croft: 'Zhang really struggling with her rhythm out there. A little bit later on the ball in this match-up today.'

Sam Smith: 'I love the tempo that Emma plays with between the points, and it never feels like she's ever knowingly rushed.'

Great service wide into Zhang's backhand, which hits it into the net. Emma wins the game to love. Three-one.

Annabel Croft: 'Very accomplished service game.'

***

Zhang's second serve is met by a massive forehand winner down the line. Love fifteen.

Zhang wins the next point on the fifth rally stroke. Fifteen all.

Emma returns into the net. Thirty fifteen.

Double fault. Thirty all.

Zhang comes in on the seventh rally stroke and wins the point with a volley that Emma can't reach two strokes later. Forty thirty.

Good ground strokes from Emma force the error and Zhang hits into the net on the eleventh rally stroke. Deuce.

This time, Zhang hits the fifth rally stroke into the net for advantage to Emma.

Sam Smith: 'This is fast and furious. This is an ambush here by an eighteen-year-old. She won't be nineteen until November. Chance for a double break here.'

Zhang wrong foots Emma with her reply to a good return. Second deuce.

Emma's return is in the net. Advantage Zhang.

Zhang hits the fifth rally stroke long. Third deuce.

Emma's return flies long. Advantage Zhang.

A longer rally. Zhang must scramble to reach Emma's crosscourt shot. It comes back at a nice height and Emma plays a forehand crosscourt winner behind Zhang. Fourth deuce.

Emma hits the fourth rally stroke into the net. Another game point for Zhang.

Double fault. Deuce number five.

Great shot from Zhang off Emma's return. Another advantage for the Chinese woman.

Emma's return catches the top of the net and Zhang hits it long. A sixth deuce.

Zhang puts the seventh rally stroke into the net and Emma has a second breakpoint.

Sam Smith: 'She has a very sweet smile, Emma, but is as tough as anything. Zhang's finding that out here.'

An amazing forehand return winner down the line. Emma has the double break. Four-one.

***

After the break, Emma to serve.

A long rally, with Zhang firing long on the tenth rally stroke. Fifteen love.

Zhang puts the fourth rally stroke into the net. The weight of Emma's ground strokes appears to be the problem. Thirty love.

Zhang hits a poor shot on the fourth rally stroke. Emma runs in and punishes it with a superb forehand volley behind the Chinese. Forty love.

Zhang hits a crosscourt forehand winner on the fourth rally stroke. Forty fifteen.

Zhang hits the sixth rally stroke into the net and Emma has another game. Five-one.

***

Zhang serving to stay in the set. A good, strong rally from both players. Emma waits for the chance to come, approaches the net, retreats to get into position and plays a backhand winner down the line behind Zhang. She looks towards her team with beaming smiles. Love fifteen.

Annabel Croft, watching a replay of the point: 'Still smiling, yeah, I think she's absolutely loving it. Just one of those sets of tennis that has been absolute perfection, hasn't it? Everything coming out of the centre of the strings, look at that lovely knee bend, staying with that through the strike. Yes, even that went in.'

Zhang hits a loopy shot off Emma's return and the Brit rushes to it and hits a stunning backhand crosscourt winner. Love thirty.

Not such a good return and Zhang is able to play a forehand pass behind Emma. Fifteen thirty.

Annabel Croft: 'You don't expect someone who has been out there on tour for well over a decade, is a top 50 player, and has been a lot better, to look this lost.'

Emma returns into the net. Thirty all.

Sam Smith: 'Yes, tactically, she does look a little lost. I'm not quite sure she knows what to do, and suppose that confidence is gone with that forehand a little bit, hasn't it? And because she's not on top of the ball at all, she's not really striking through the middle of it.'

Emma's return flies long. Forty thirty.

Emma's hits wide on the fourth rally stroke. Game to Zhang. Five-two.

***

Emma serving for the set.

Zhang's return is overhit. Fifteen love.

Good steady ground strokes from Emma, and Zhang hits long on the thirteenth rally stroke. Thirty love.

Emma hits the fifth rally stroke down the line behind Zhang. Forty love.

Sam Smith: 'Yes! Well, we knew something was in the air when, just over half an hour ago, she came out and broke Zhang to love. Three set points for the eighteen-year-old.'

Emma hits a massive backhand crosscourt winner off Zhang's return to take the game to love and win the first set. Six-two.

***

Tim Henman, courtside: 'Well, first things first. Phenomenal set of tennis from Emma. They have very similar games, but Emma is just beating her opponent to the punch, serving so consistently from the back of the court, playing aggressively and making no unforced errors, but this is where the challenge comes. Emma comes onto the court with nothing to lose against a much higher ranked opponent. The psychology now changes—she has something to lose. I expect a reaction from Zhang. She's a top fifty player. She has been around for a long, long time so it's really important in these early stages of the second set that Emma can try to maintain the momentum. So, if we're going to see a change, this is where we'll probably see it, but an absolutely brilliant start. So far, so good.'

Zhang looks decidedly miserable as she comes back onto court ten to serve at the beginning of the second set.

Emma hits the eighth rally stroke into the net and expresses annoyance with herself. Fifteen love.

Same again, but on the tenth rally stroke this time. The ground strokes seem fine, deep, and powerful, so both lost points were unforced errors. Thirty love.

Zhang hits into the net on the fifth rally stroke. Thirty fifteen.

Emma's return skips off the top of the net and lands on the line, wrong-footing Zhang. Sorry, not sorry. Thirty all.

Emma hits an amazing backhand defensive shot on the fourth rally stroke. It lands in the very corner of the court and Zhang's crosscourt forehand shot flies wide. Breakpoint. Thirty forty.

Annabel Croft: 'I think Zhang hesitated, didn't she? In the previous match-up, she would have come forward on that, taking the ball out of the air. She backpedals [this time], got herself into difficulties and made an error. Just looks as if she's really a little lost.'

Zhang pounces on a short return from Emma and hits behind the Brit. Deuce.

Double fault gives Emma another breakpoint.

The serve shoots off the line and Emma's return flies wide. Deuce.

A genuinely deep, wide serve from Zhang, which Emma returns long, shouting out in frustration. Advantage Zhang.

A good, deep return into Zhang's forehand makes the Chinese player hit long. Third deuce.

Emma plays the return and the fourth rally stroke deep into Zhang's forehand corner, the second one winning the point. Breakpoint again. Advantage Emma.

Sam Smith: 'Relentless pressure from Raducanu.'

Zhang puts Emma's return into the net. Another break. One-love.

Sam Smith: 'All momentum now with the eighteen year old and she's pretty much winning in every department, isn't she, Annabel?'

Annabel Croft: 'Really is. When you look at the different rally lengths. Under five, Raducanu winning twenty-three of those, but winning seven out of eight points over nine, and those are the psychological points, aren't they, when the rally gets a little bit extended, you're kind of eating into each other's psyche, and she's winning pretty much most of those, so that's going to hurt. That was such an important game to try to get through, and for Zhang, it was equally as important, and it went in the other direction. Emma's not put a foot wrong in this match.'

* * *

Emma serves. A good rally from both players, but Emma hits into the net on the ninth rally stroke. Love fifteen.

Sam Smith: 'That's only the third point she has lost behind her [first] serve in the match.'

Emma shuffles wider on the service line and hits a great serve into Zhang's backhand, pulling the error from the return, which flies long. Fifteen all.

Emma hits Zhang's return into the net. Fifteen thirty.

A good, deep second serve sees Zhang's return fly long. Thirty all.

A five-stroke rally. Emma comes into the net to punish a loopy ball and smashes a forehand winner, leaving Zhang stranded. Forty thirty.

Sam Smith: 'She doesn't miss those!'

Annabel Croft: 'Really quick to move up the court to take that out of the air, especially on this kind of surface. Very difficult for a player to catch up in a rally if you take the ball on the fly like that.'

Ace down the T. Two-love.

***

Zhang serving. Emma wins the point on the fourth rally stroke with a crosscourt backhand. Love fifteen.

Emma puts the fourth rally stroke into the net. Fifteen all.

Emma's return lands right on the baseline. Zhang thinks it is out and hits into the net. Fifteen thirty.

Sam Smith: 'Must admit, strange, looked a little long. The replay shows it must have just hit the back edge of the line. It's another example of how confident Raducanu is hitting the ball, when you're hitting all the lines like this.'

An eleven-stroke rally. Zhang comes into the net and her volley clips the net cord and wins the point. Thirty all.

Emma hits the fourth rally stroke long. Forty thirty.

A brilliant backhand winner down the line from Emma on the fourth rally stroke. Deuce.

Emma has Zhang running back and forth then comes into the net and hits a backhand crosscourt volley finding the space where Zhang isn't. Breakpoint.

Sam Smith: 'This is so well played. Not able to do anything, unfortunately.'

Annabel Croft, watching the replay: '[Zhang's] reaction says it all, doesn't it? Almost like she has no idea what to do in this match, I mean that one hitting the line as well. Look how the ball travels away from her opponent, and then so good to move up the court here, sensing where her opponent is. Great court craft.'

A wide ace. Second deuce.

Zhang hits a forehand winner down the line on the seventh rally stroke. Advantage to the Chinese player.

Sam Smith: 'Wow! Where did that come from. All the frustration going into that forehand.'

Emma hits an even better backhand crosscourt return. Deuce number three.

Emma hits the eighth rally stroke as a lob. Zhang scampers back, but it falls just long. Advantage Zhang.

Zhang hits Emma's return into the net. Fourth deuce.

A great forehand crosscourt winner from Zhang on the seventh stroke of the rally. Advantage to her again.

Emma's return is put into the net by Zhang. Emma shouts at her team box. Deuce number five.

Good, deep return from Emma and Zhang hits it wide and long. Second breakpoint.

Annabel Croft: 'She has court presence and charisma. Another breakpoint in this game.'

Emma hits the fourth rally stroke into Zhang's backhand corner. Game to Emma.

Sam Smith: 'It's a double break for Raducanu as she dominates in this second-round match.'

Three-love.

**

Emma serving.

Zhang hits the eighth rally stroke into the net. Fifteen love.

Unreturnable serve. Thirty love.

Emma hits a forehand winner down the line off Zhang's return. Forty love.

Zhang returns wide and Emma is four love up.

Sam Smith: 'Zhang is becoming more and more ragged by the second, down the other end, and her walk's got a little slower, as well.'

Annabel Croft: 'This is an annihilation.'

Four-love.

**

Zhang serving.

60

Emma puts the sixth rally stroke into the net. Fifteen love.

Good shot from Zhang off Emma's return wrongfoots the Brit. Thirty love.

The crowd shouts a collective 'ooh!'as Emma's forehand return finds the very corner of the court. Amazing shot. Thirty fifteen.

Super forehand down the line by Zhang off Emma's return. Forty fifteen.

Sam Smith: 'Zhang's just feeding on the scraps out here. They haven't even been on court an hour.'

Zhang hits Emma's return very wide. Forty thirty.

Sam Smith: 'Looks like she's playing with a little sort of dark cloud above her head at the moment. She's not enjoying this at all.'

Emma hits the tenth rally stroke into the net. Game to Zhang. Four-one.

***

Emma serves and the return flies long. Fifteen love.

Ace down the T. Thirty love.

Zhang smashes a winner on the thirteenth stroke of the rally. She seems to have a new determination. Thirty fifteen.

Annabel Croft: 'There's not been too many opportunities when she's been able to get Raducanu onto the back foot and into a defensive position.'

Zhang puts the fourth rally stroke into the net. Forty fifteen.

Rare error from Emma off Zhang's return. Forty thirty.

Good shot on the fourth rally stroke gives Zhang deuce. Emma seems to have lost concentration a little.

Zhang gets Emma out of position and plays a backhand crosscourt winner on the eighth rally stroke. Breakpoint.

Annabel Croft: 'There's been a mini shift in how the rallies have been playing in the last few. Just being a little bit closer to the baseline, starting to get her rhythm going at the back. Can she build on it, I wonder?'

Emma puts the seventh rally stroke into the net. Zhang breaks for the first time. Is this a shift in the match? Four-two.

Annabel Croft: 'Perhaps there was just a little bit pulling back from Raducanu in that last game. Just wasn't quite going after shots as much. You can understand it—closer to that finish line, thinking about things a little bit more. It's getting Zhang a tiny bit of a lifeline.'

Sam Smith: 'A small shift.'

Annabel Croft: 'A very small shift on court ten.'

***

Zhang to serve.

Double fault. Love fifteen.

Emma's return into the net. Fifteen all.

A wonderful backhand down the line winner from Emma on the fourth rally stroke. She fist-pumps towards her team. Fifteen thirty.

Emma hits the tenth rally stroke into the net. One of the best rallies of the match. Emma looks exasperated at her team. Thirty all.

Annabel Croft: 'It's really been an uphill battle for her [Zhang], but she's just starting to get stuck into a little bit more of the rallies. She's giving Raducanu a lot more to think about and starting to make her feel a little less comfortable.'

A deep, wide serve from Zhang and Emma's return flies wide. Forty thirty.

Zhang hits wide off Emma's return. Deuce.

Emma's very deep return is hit into the net. Advantage Emma. Breakpoint.

On the fifth rally stroke, Zhang hits a winning forehand behind Emma. Deuce two.

Zhang hits the seventh rally stroke long and wide off a deep ground stroke from Emma. Breakpoint two.

Going for too much, Emma hits the sixth rally stroke just wide. She screams in annoyance. Third deuce.

Zhang hits wide off Emma's return. Breakpoint three.

Good wide shot from Zhang forces Emma to hit the ninth rally stroke into the net. Fourth deuce.

Emma is puffing and leaning on her racquet at the end of the point.

Emma hits the fourth rally stroke high and long. Advantage Zhang.

Emma's return into the net for the third game in a row for the Chinese player. Four-three.

***

Emma serves and Zhang returns into the net. Fifteen love.

Sam Smith: 'Eighty-four percent first serves won. That's exceptional.'

Zhang skies the return. Thirty love.

Sam Smith: 'That's another one right there.'

Zhang hits the eighteenth stroke of the rally high and wide after a good, hard-hitting point. Forty love.

Wide ace. An important hold for the Brit. Five-three.

***

Zhang serving to stay in the match.

A great start for Emma. Zhang mishits the eleventh rally stroke. Love fifteen.

Emma digs deep on the fourth rally stroke and the ball flies long. Fifteen all.

A wayward shot off Emma's return sails wide and long. Fifteen thirty.

Good serve. Emma's return is high and Zhang, rushing the net, plays a forehand volley into the empty court. Thirty all.

Zhang has Emma scampering back and forth and makes her hit the eighth rally stroke into the net. Forty thirty.

Emma's return long. She's going to have to serve for the match. Five-four.

***

Sam Smith: 'Serving, in the sun, for a place in the third round.'

Zhang hits the tenth rally stroke into the net, trying to hit a dropshot from the back of the court. Fifteen love.

63

Sam Smith: 'What does Zhang need to do?'

Annabel Croft: 'I think she needs to try and play the way that she's been playing in the last few games, which is to hang in the rallies, try to get on top of the point to retarget that forehand, but move the ball around so that she's on top of the rally. Not sure where that decision for the dropshot came from.'

Emma screams as she overhits the ninth rally stroke. Fifteen all.

Good backhand winner from Emma on the fifth rally stroke. Thirty fifteen.

There is some sort of massed drum band practice coming from just off court.

Sam Smith: 'Amidst the din, she's got to somehow block it all out.'

Zhang's return is long. Perhaps the noise is affecting both of them. Match point.

A long match point rally at forty fifteen, sees Zhang hit long on the fourteenth rally stroke. Emma throws down her racquet, bends double and holds her face.

Sam Smith: 'She can't believe it! Raducanu books a place in the third round, still yet to drop a set. She beats Zhang in straight sets, six two, six four.'

***

Emma waves at the crowd, thanks Zhang for the game, before smiling and laughing, and running over to her team where she receives hugs from each of them, eventually collecting her racquet from the back of the court.

Tim Henman, courtside: 'It's absolutely fantastic. I could not be more impressed with Raducanu's performance. Two elements—the quality of her tennis to be up six two, four love, she was absolutely faultless. She made so few unforced errors, completely dominated her opponent, but you are always expecting an experienced player to respond, and Zhang did that. She got back to four three and the other element that really impressed me with Raducanu, was the way that she dealt with that adversity. There was absolutely no panic. She showed so much composure, just to regroup and played a very strong service game at four three to go up five three and then serving it out. It's hot, the sun's in her eyes, and then we get a marching band just on the outskirts of the court making so much noise, but she kept her focus, and it is an absolutely brilliant win for her.'

Third round next against Sara Sorribes Tormo.

6 Sara Sorribes Tormo—U.S. Open Round Three

Sara is Spanish and ranked forty-one in the world, so yet another step up for Emma. She stands five feet nine inches and is twenty-four years old. She won the Guadalajara tournament in March.

It's sunny, seventy-five Fahrenheit with low humidity, so ideal for tennis. The players are out on court seventeen. Emma in her signature red and blue slam outfit, yellow visor and white shoes. Sara is in a neon-chartreuse top, white skirt and blue shoes. She's not wearing a hat or visor and has her hair tied in a topknot. Both players are using Wilson racquets.

Anne Keothavong[xi]: 'She [Emma] really has had an incredible run, just going from strength to strength, but I don't think anyone could have predicted the kind of run she's gone on over the past few months.'

Sam Smith: 'She won three rounds of qualifying, didn't drop a set and has gone through two very experienced players. Vögele and Zhang, both top fifty players, but this is the highest ranked player at forty-one that she has ever faced.'

As they finish warmup on court seventeen, we see Andrew Richardson, Emma's coach, Wil Herbert, the physio, and Chris Helliar, her agent, in Emma's team box. Emma won the toss and elected to serve. The winner of this match will play the world number one, Ash Barty or Shelby Rogers who are to play later in the day.

Emma to serve. Sorribes Tormo returns into the net. Fifteen love.

Double fault. Fifteen all.

Sorribes Tormo grunts belatedly on every point. Emma makes an unforced error, hitting into the net on the ninth rally stroke. Fifteen thirty.

Sorribes Tormo's return is high, and Emma hits a winning forehand down the line off it. Thirty all.

Emma fires a hard shot into Sorribes Tormo's forehand off the return of serve and the Spaniard hits long. Forty thirty.

Deep serve into Sorribes Tormo's backhand sets the tone and the Spaniard hits into the net on the fourth rally stroke. Game to Emma. One game to love.

***

Sam Smith: 'How do you think she's gonna deal with the different types of spins out there that she's going to face and the presence of Sorribes Tormo, who has got this sort of delayed grunt here, and there's a lot going on, isn't there, at the other end of the court, including the neon top.'

Anne Keothavong: 'Yeah. To be perfectly honest, I'm not sure, because I've never seen her play against anyone with this type of style before, but I know she will have done her homework. I know she would have watched video footage of her opponent yesterday. She's very good at the old homework and research. I think we love the fact that she does most of it herself.'

The Spaniard serves. On the eighth rally stroke, Emma hits long. Fifteen love.

Again, Emma hits the eighth rally stroke long. Thirty love.

A second serve is punished by a huge forehand crosscourt return, which makes Sorribes Tormo hit her shot high. Emma's into the net like a flash and volleys a forehand winner into the open part of the court. Thirty fifteen.

A rally starts to build, but Emma hits a backhand crosscourt winner on the eighth rally stroke. Thirty all.

Again, a good rally, with Sorribes Tormo mixing up the shots, but Emma, inside the baseline, hits a backhand winner down the line. Breakpoint. Thirty forty.

Emma's shot on the eighth rally stroke clips the net to Sorribes Tormo's benefit. Emma gets to the next shot, but the Spaniard has come into the net and hits the volley into the open court. Deuce.

Sorribes Tormo hits the fifth rally stroke into the net. Breakpoint again.

Emma's return is a fraction long. Deuce number two.

Long return again. Advantage Sorribes Tormo.

During the next rally, Emma pins Sorribes Tormo into the backhand corner then fires a forehand winner behind her opponent. Deuce three.

Anne Keothavong: 'She seems to have exceptional clarity about what she wants to do.'

On the seventeenth rally stroke, Sorribes Tormo plays a dropshot. Emma is fast enough to get to it but plays the shot a fraction long. She walks back to the baseline, telling herself off. Advantage Sorribes Tormo.

Sorribes Tormo hits the fifth rally stroke well long. Deuce number four.

A rather wild return from Emma flies wide. Advantage Sorribes Tormo again.

A good return is hit into the net by the Spaniard. Fifth deuce.

Another excellent return and Sorribes Tormo mishits wide. Breakpoint number three.

The longest rally of the match and Emma puts the pressure on from about rally stroke fourteen. She gets Sorribes Tormo off-balance and forces her to hit into the net on the nineteenth rally stroke. Emma has the break. Two-love.

***

Emma serves and Sorribes Tormo hits the sixth stroke long. Fifteen love.

Double fault. Fifteen all.

A second double fault. A very rare occurrence for Emma. Fifteen thirty.

Terrific deep wide serve. Sorribes Tormo hits the sixth rally stroke into the net. Thirty all.

Sorribes Tormo hits the tenth rally stroke slightly wide. Forty thirty.

Sorribes Tormo hits the return long. Game to Emma. A good recovery and hold. Three-love.

Sorribes Tormo serves, and Emma hits a simply fantastic return that lands at her feet making her mishit into the net. Love fifteen.

Emma hits the eighth rally stroke long. Fifteen all.

Sorribes Tormo hits the fifteenth rally stroke long. Fifteen thirty.

Sam Smith: 'At the moment, Sorribes Tormo is being outplayed in these baseline rallies.'

Anne Keothavong: 'Sorribes Tormo's struggling to deal with Emma's weight of shot out here.'

Massively heavy ground strokes from inside the baseline by Emma. She bides her time, then hits a forehand volley which the Spaniard can only hit into the net. Two breakpoints. Fifteen forty.

Emma tries to go for too much and hits the fourth rally stroke wide. Still breakpoint. Thirty forty.

Sorribes Tormo puts the eleventh rally stroke into the net. Game to Emma. Now four games to love.

Sam Smith: 'Wow! Another break.'

***

Emma serving. Sorribes Tormo hits the twentieth rally stroke into the net. Fifteen love.

Sam Smith: 'Tormo seems rather lost, struggling to find a way past the eighteen-year-old. Putting the ball back into play isn't going to get the job done out here.'

Emma hits the Spaniard's return with a vicious backhand tight to the backhand line. Sorribes Tormo returns it, only to find that Emma has arrived at the net to produce a backhand volley into the same location, wrong-footing her opponent. Thirty love.

The Spaniard's return flies long. Forty love.

Great second serve and Sorribes Tormo's return flies wide. Emma's game to love. Five-love.

***

Fabulous crosscourt return of a second serve from the Spaniard. Love fifteen.

Sorribes Tormo can't get her racquet to the fifth rally stroke and mishits wide. Love thirty.

Massive forehand return passes Sorribes Tormo. Three set points to Emma. Love forty.

On the sixth rally stroke, Emma hits a backhand down the line to break to love and give Sara Sorribes Tormo a New York bagel. Six-love.

***

Sam Smith: 'It is a demolition. Raducanu's given Sorribes Tormo a bagel, the Brit taking the first set by six games to love. Tim, you've hardly had time to put your sun cream on, can she keep playing at this level?'

Tim Henman, courtside: 'Yes, she can. I mean, it's an absolute ball-striking clinic. We talked about the baseline exchanges where Raducanu has got the weight of shot, but it is also on the return of serve. Raducanu is just absolutely killing the serve, and you know, it is the perfect start. She's one set at six love, she's playing great tennis, but is only one set so this is where you would expect, you know, the experienced player to be able to turn it round in the beginning of the second set, so hopefully Raducanu can maintain that.'

Emma to serve in the second set.

Sorribes Tormo struggles to return wide, but Emma pounces upon it and volleys a forehand winner into the open court. Fifteen love.

Emma hits a forehand winner down the line off the Spaniard's less than perfect return. It lands squarely on the baseline. Thirty love.

A poor shot on the fifth rally stroke sees Emma hit into the net. Thirty fifteen.

On the seventh rally stroke, Emma overhits the ground stroke and it goes long. Unforced error again. Thirty all.

Sam Smith: 'When you've won the opening set six love, I mean, the key for any player who has, just done that is to maintain their focus and concentration at the start of the second set, which is easier said than done. Can be dangerous when you've beaten a very good player so easily. It's like a big point here, for Emma.'

A great one-two. Emma sends Sorribes Tormo scampering to reach a deep, wide first serve, then has time to fire a backhand into the open court. She screams out, 'Yeah! Come on!' Forty thirty.

Emma hits a deep shot off the Spaniard's return. Her reply comes high over the net where Emma is waiting. She smashes a forehand shot into the vacant court. One game to love.

***

Sam Smith: 'Seventh game to zero now. Utterly dominant.'

The Spaniard with new balls. Straight away, Emma has Sorribes Tormo overreaching and she hits the fifth rally stroke into the net. Love fifteen.

Again, Sorribes Tormo is being stretched, and this time, she hits the fifth rally stroke wide on Emma's forehand side. Love thirty.

Anne Keothavong: 'She looks lost out here. She needs time on the ball which Raducanu's not giving her. I'm surprised I haven't seen her trying to moon ball a few more on the forehand wing, just to try to push Emma further back.'

Sorribes Tormo tries serving and volleying and manages to win the point at the net on the seventh rally stroke. Fifteen thirty.

This time, Emma is at the net at the earliest opportunity and smashes the sixth rally point for a winner. Two breakpoints. Fifteen forty.

A massive return is sent back with interest, and Emma's reply stops at the net cord. She shakes her head as she paces up and down the back of the court. Thirty forty.

Emma hits a backhand winner down the line on the sixteenth rally stroke. Another break of serve. Eight games in a row now. Two-love.

Sam Smith: 'The Spaniard is in the trenches right now.'

***

Emma serves and hits Sorribes Tormo's return long. Love fifteen.

Again, trying to push too hard, Emma hits the seventh rally stroke long. Love thirty.

Unforced error by Sorribes Tormo, hitting the net on the thirteenth rally stroke. Fifteen thirty.

Sam Smith: 'Again, she's got this great tempo, hasn't she, between the points. She doesn't take too long, but she's not rushing about either. She's the one in control out there.'

Sorribes Tormo skies the return long. Thirty all.

Emma hits her serve deep and wide into Sorribes Tormo's forehand side. The return is weak and loopy, and Emma smashes a forehand winner into the open court. Forty thirty.

Sorribes Tormo hits long on the fourth rally stroke. Game to Emma. Three-love.

***

Sam Smith: 'Out on court seventeen, Tim, you've been across the net of the greats of the game like Sampras, you know, wonderful players and we're seeing Emma here, right at the start of her career. I think the great players have a presence. Can you describe what it's like seeing Emma on court?'

Tim Henman courtside: 'Yeah, she's put in an absolutely faultless performance, and we talk a lot about psychology and sport, and the most basic form of psychology is staying in the present, and that is so important that Emma does that right now. Yes, she's won nine games in a row but that's in the past, and we all know that the finish line is potentially only three games away, but what she's got to do is just keep knuckling down, playing one point at a time, controlled aggression has been absolutely spot on as her opponent is just not hurting her, so she can stay in the rallies, wait for opportunities, and she has just been picking her off absolutely brilliantly. So, more of the same, and you know, fingers crossed, she can get the job done.'

Sam Smith: 'From where you're standing, do you think Emma has the charisma and the presence of a potential top player?'

Tim Henman: 'Yeah, there's no doubt, I mean, whatever happens in this match, in this tournament, we really are watching a star of the future.'

Sorribes Tormo sat with her head in her hands during the break. She comes out to serve with a new determination.

On the seventeenth rally stroke of the first rally, she manages to play a winner close to Emma's forehand line. Fifteen love.

She's waving at the crowd to support her, but Emma continues to fire amazing groundstrokes, waiting for the right opportunities.

Emma's return is in the net. Thirty love.

Better return from Emma and Sorribes Tormo can only swat it into the net. Thirty fifteen.

Emma's talking to herself and nodding that she knows what to do. She has Sorribes Tormo on the run again and the Spaniard hits long on the seventh stroke of the rally. Thirty all.

Emma's return only just misses the net and Sorribes Tormo dashes in to play into Emma's backhand side, but the Brit is way too fast and hits a backhand crosscourt passing shot to bring up breakpoint. Thirty forty.

Sam Smith: 'There's more misery here for Sorribes Tormo.'

Emma can't return a great serve. Deuce.

On the eleventh rally stroke, Emma comes in and fires a forehand volley winner past the Spaniard. Advantage Emma.

Sam Smith: 'This is a demolition.'

Emma has the Spaniard running again and she hits the seventh rally stroke into the net. Emma breaks again. An unbelievable ten consecutive games. Four love.

***

Sam Smith: 'She keeps going. The look on Tormo's face says everything. Anne, you've been around her in the fed

73

cup[xii], I mean, she's very young, she's inexperienced, and I'm stunned the level of intensity out here. It has not dropped for a second, has it?'

Anne Keothavong: 'Oh, this performance has really taken my breath away, but still some finishing off to do.'

Sam Smith: 'We all knew she was good.'

Anne Keothavong: 'That's an understatement, but I don't think anyone could have predicted that run at Wimbledon and this hardcourt season she's having out here in the States.'

Sam Smith: 'Don't forget, she didn't play during the pandemic at all.'

Emma serving. The return is loopy and misses the baseline. Fifteen love.

Emma hits the return into the net. Fifteen all.

A great one-two. Deep, wide serve to Sorribes Tormo's forehand, then she punishes the return with a backhand crosscourt winner. Thirty fifteen.

Sorribes Tormo hits the fourth rally stroke long. Forty fifteen.

An almost identical point to the fourth, but this time it is a forehand winner down the line. Game to Emma. Five-love.

Sam Smith: 'She is almost there.'

***

Sorribes Tormo comes out to serve.

Sam Smith: 'Take a look at that six love, five love score line against a player who beat Ash Barty [world number one] at the Olympics only last month—Sorribes Tormo. It's been a torment out here for the Spaniard, now serving to stay in this third round.'

On the fourteenth rally stroke, Emma plays an outrageous forehand winner behind Sorribes Tormo. Love fifteen.

Sam Smith: 'Emma, don't wake up. Wherever you are, stay there!'

Sorribes Tormo hits the fifth rally stroke wide. Love thirty.

Anne Keothavong: 'I can't believe she is a point away from double-bageling the world number forty-one.'

Sam Smith: 'Sorribes Tormo was very much the favourite coming into this match.'

The Spaniard manages to get a crosscourt winner on the seventh stroke of the rally. Fifteen thirty.

Great serve down the T, which Emma can only return into the net. Thirty all.

Sam Smith: 'Sorribes Tormo trying to prise a game out of Raducanu here.'

Emma's return goes long. She skips along the baseline in annoyance. Forty thirty.

Emma runs in and volleys the eighth rally stroke into the open side of the court. Deuce.

Tiring, Sorribes Tormo hits the eleventh rally stroke into the net and Emma has match point.

An uncharacteristic wild swipe return from Emma returns the score to deuce.

Sam Smith: 'Let's just forget that one.'

The longest rally of the match gives the Spaniard the advantage as Emma hits the twenty-second rally stroke long.

Emma hits a huge forehand return down the line. Back to deuce.

Emma hits the sixteenth rally stroke wide. Advantage to the Spaniard.

Emma plays a great shot into the corner of the court and Sorribes Tormo hits it long on the fifth rally stroke. Deuce number four.

Emma hits the tenth rally stroke long. Advantage Sorribes Tormo.

Emma's return comes high over the net and Sorribes Tormo smashes it into the open court. She's saved the double-bagel and the crowd cheer loudly. Five-one.

***

Emma is going to have to serve for the match and a place in the fourth round.

Emma hits the fifth rally shot into the net cord. Love fifteen.

Very hard-hitting rally and Sorribes Tormo hits the sixth rally stroke into the net. Fifteen all.

The Spaniard skies the return off Emma's second serve. Thirty fifteen.

Trying to slice, Emma hits the seventeenth rally stroke into the net. Is she getting nervy? Thirty all.

Sorribes Tormo returns into the net. Forty thirty. Second match point.

A great serve down the T, which Sorribes Tormo returns towards Emma who has time to step aside and play a fabulous forehand down the line winner. Game set and match to Emma Raducanu. She's in the fourth round of the U.S. Open, six love, six one.

She throws her arms up into the air, and a wonderful laughing smile plays over her face.

Sam Smith: 'Raducanu delivers a New York masterclass.'

Emma collects her towel and the posing for selfies begins with hefty security guards standing by.

***

Sam Smith: 'Anne, as GB team captain, you must be jumping for joy.'

Anne Keothavong: 'I'm absolutely beaming. That was just an outstanding performance from Emma Raducanu from start to finish. There was just no let up. She got a tiny little bit tight trying to close it out, but that's understandable. That's okay.'

Sam Smith: 'I think her expression says it all, but for Emma Raducanu it's onwards and upwards, and I can tell you, whether it's Barty [world number one] or Rogers who she'll watch tonight, she will not be on court seventeen next week.'

Emma speaks live courtside, to Karthi Gnanasegaram, with fans cheering behind her.

Karthi Gnanasegaram: 'Emma, you're just waving to the crowd who absolutely love you. Congratulations, you're into the last sixteen of a second Grand Slam. That was so impressive. Six love, six one. The commentators really didn't know what to say. What was going through your mind during that match?'

Emma: 'I mean, I was playing very well, and I know Sara is an extremely tough opponent. I mean, she doesn't make a mistake, so you have to be on your game every single point, and I had to work so hard and there were some really, really long deuce games that could have gone either way. So, I'm just really happy that I managed to maintain and stay on it, and win in the end.'

Karthi Gnanasegaram: 'She's one of the most awkward and consistent players to face on the tour. You talk about how your mental strength and your preparation is one of your keys. How did you plan for this match?'

Emma: 'Honestly, for this one, I knew that the plan was I had to hit through her—I had to hit the corners. I mean, if you trade against her you're probably going to come out second best, so I just took the game to her and I hit more winners than errors today.'

Karthi Gnanasegaram: 'I know you're enjoying being in New York, but you're in the fourth round of a Grand Slam for the second successive time. How are you coping with all of this? It's quite a whirlwind, isn't it?'

Emma: 'I've got a great team around me, a great team here, so we're just sticking to the same routines, and it's been two weeks in New York now and into the third week. I never thought I'd be here, but I'm just so, so excited, and yeah, recover tomorrow, and then back on it on Monday into the second week of the Grand Slam.'

Karthi Gnanasegaram talking over the fans shouting for Emma: 'People clearly want selfies and some autographs from you, but you might be playing the world number one Ash Barty or world forty-three, Shelby Rogers. This court is the pit, court seventeen. You're likely to be on a very big court for that. How are you enjoying the experience of the crowd in New York?'

Emma: 'The crowd is so amazing, so I want to thank them, [she turns to wave at them all] actually everyone, thank you so much honestly, like they helped me through so many moments.'

Huge applause drowns her out.

Karthi Gnanasegaram: 'I'll let you get back to them coz they clearly want to say thank you to you.'

Emma: 'Well, thank you so much.' And she continues signing yellow and blue giant tennis balls, peaked caps, flags and standing for selfies.

Tim Henman, also courtside, watching the adoring fans mobbing Emma: 'Yeah, it was brilliant. There's been people sort of streaming out past us basically just going 'wow'. It was that good a performance from Raducanu against a much more experienced opponent. She had a very clear game plan and she needed that in these baseline exchanges. Raducanu was just clinical in waiting for the opportunity to unload on the shots and it was such an accomplished performance for someone who is so inexperienced at this level.'

Catherine Whitaker, in the studio: 'It was actually quite reassuring to see her get ever so slightly tight, just for a point or two at the end of that match, Tim, coz it was reassuring that she is, in fact, human. I'm just trying to put it into context for us how unusual and breathtaking it is to see an eighteen year old put in that kind of performance on this kind of an occasion'

Tim Henman: 'Yeah, you're absolutely right, Catherine. There are two elements—there's the level of performance that she was able to maintain with the consistency and to be aggressive, but also the awareness of the way that she played because she didn't always just pull the trigger, second, third, fourth shots into the rally. She sometimes constructed, using heavy spin sometimes when Sorribes Tormo was using the heavy slice and when she got the opportunity to unload, she went for it. As is the case with these great players, they find a way, and for her to win six love, six one to go into the fourth round of a slam, it is going to be good for her confidence.'

Catherine Whitaker: 'I had to just look down at my notes and check that was actually right, Tim, just hearing it out loud sounds so ridiculous. How many phones do you think there are in New York City with pictures of Emma Raducanu right now?'

Tim Henman: 'This has been a great court, court seventeen. It has such a good atmosphere is like a mini amphitheatre and she's definitely picked up probably another three thousand fans today, and what's exciting is, yeah, as you mentioned, she's not going to be on this court in the next round. She's going to be on an even bigger court, and irrespective of the result in the fourth round, she will gain many, many more fans for the future.'

Catherine Whitaker: 'If you allow us to get ahead of ourselves just for the last question, Tim, it will almost certainly be the Arthur Ashe Stadium and it will most likely be against the world number one Ash Barty. With all due respect to her opponent, Shelby Rogers. Does Emma Raducanu have a chance?'

Tim Henman: 'Yeah, she has a chance, I mean, you know, everybody's got a chance in a two-horse race but it's going to be a massive step up in class. She's certainly been the form player of this year. Ash Barty is number one in the world for a reason. She's won in Cincinnati, she won at Wimbledon, and that was, you know, clear for everyone to see, but what's important is that Raducanu, whoever she plays, is able to make sure that she sticks to her game plan. And if she is going to play on a big court, one of the advantages that she can get out there, hopefully, have a practice session just to get used to the conditions, before she goes out there for the match itself. But first things first, it's important that she enjoys this, savours the moment before she thinks about the round of sixteen.'

Catherine Whitaker: 'She'll have to leave the court first, Tim. She might spend the next forty-eight hours signing autographs on court seventeen. I'll let you go and get in the queue for another Raducanu autograph. It might take you a while to get it, Tim. We're going to just soak up these scenes for as long as we possibly can. Annabel.'

Annabel Croft in the studio: 'I think she's going to sign every single autograph down there. Why not savour this moment and as she keeps on saying, she's really appreciated the support that she's had on this court and they probably followed her from a couple of days ago as well, so why not give them something back and, I think, go for it. She is really picking up, as Tim said, thousands of fans every time she plays. Emma's tennis was just breathtaking.'

Greg Rusedski: 'She's got everything, I mean, I look at her intensity, her focus and also the variety in her game. I haven't seen her coming forward in a match so often. Rallies were brutal. They were long, averaging about six point five shots and she was just tactically so astute, because to play in this manner at such an important moment in your career is so, so impressive. At eighteen years old, for me this is the biggest story in the women's game right now, I would say, because of that performance, I can't wait for the match against Barty, the world number one, coming up next.'

Annabel Croft: 'If you take away the fact she's British, if you're watching a performance like this, you would say this is one of the most sensational performances of a breakout onto the tour. The fact that she's carried it on from what we saw at Wimbledon and being able to maintain that momentum and actually improve several notches since we saw her at Wimbledon, I mean, this is absolutely mesmerising tennis that we're seeing from her. To blitz and blast and pummel a real kind of tough, tricky opponent in Sorribes Tormo, she didn't give her a chance. I feel sorry for her.'

Greg Rusedski: 'And also Sorribes Tormo beat a certain Ash Barty at the Olympics, so that just puts you kind of in a good stead to think, hey the world's her oyster right now, and what I loved is she dealt so well with the variety of the slices, the mixes of height. Her footwork was exceptional. She just did everything right. It was relentless from start to finish, and yes, there was a fractional hiccup, but the hiccup came when her opponent was serving, not when she served for the match.'

7 Shelby Rogers—U.S. Open Round Four

All the talk and anticipation of Emma facing world number one, Ash Barty, came to nothing. Twenty-eight-year-old American, Shelby Rogers, the world number forty-three, shocked the tennis world by beating Barty, 6-2, 1-6, 7-6 in a last set tiebreak, which she won 7-5. Without doubt, the home crowd spurred her on.

Emma was not to face Ash Barty after all. Probably that was good for the Bromley teenager. It might have stopped the fairy tale at a stroke. We'll never know and, after winning the Australian Open in 2022, Ashleigh Barty[xiii] retired from professional tennis, meaning that the two would now never meet.

Players can only ever play the person on the other side of the net. The stage was set for a round four match with Shelby Rogers in the world's biggest tennis stadium—the Arthur Ashe Court at Flushing Meadows, with its capacity of over twenty-three thousand spectators.

The players came out on court, following a huge match that had just completed. The seats had therefore emptied, and this might work in the Bromley girl's favour, removing some of the pressure of having to perform on this enormous stage. It would gradually refill during the early part of the match.

Emma was wearing her now familiar red and blue NY slam tennis outfit with the yellow sun visor. Shelby Rogers wore a pale arctic blue tennis dress and white shoes. Her hair was in a ponytail, but she had opted not to wear a hat or visor.

Martina Navratilova[xiv], commentator: 'Shelby Rogers [an American] is favourite to win this match, but the crowd, even if she has any kind of let down, the crowd will carry her through here, so she'll be ready. This is such an opportunity. She's worked so hard to get to this point. That was the biggest win of her career, *ever*, two days ago [beating Barty] and she's been around for too long to be sitting on the roses after that match, so should be ready to go. This is a fantastic opportunity for Shelby Rogers to get the furthest she's ever been.'

Tim Henman, courtside: 'If I had to pick a winner, I'd go with Emma Raducanu. I think they both are looking a bit nervous and that's to be expected. It's a big match, a big opportunity. For me, one of the areas with Rogers is footwork. I don't think she's the best mover, and when you are a little nervous that is affected even more. If Emma can get her feet moving early on, get up those small steps in and around the court and start to work Rogers side to side, sometimes, go back behind her to open up the holes, because if she gets the opportunity, Raducanu can step in and dictate play from the back of the court. That's when I feel she's going to be at her most dangerous.'

Catherine Whitaker, in the studio: 'How important is the start of this match for Emma?'

Tim Henman: 'Yeah, I think it is. This is probably the biggest match of her life having come through qualifying. She's on a huge stage. She has a little bit more experience than at Wimbledon, so, yeah, she can stamp her authority. If we reflect on the third-round match, we wanted her to stamp her authority there and she won the first eleven games against Sorribes Tormo, so I don't think we can quite expect that today, but a good start is certainly preferable.'

Emma won the toss and elected to serve.

Fault, then Rogers hits the second serve into the net. Fifteen, love.

A longer rally, with Rogers winning the point with a cross court shot behind Emma on the tenth rally stroke. Fifteen all.

Rogers hits the fourth rally stroke long. Thirty fifteen.

Another first serve, but Emma hits a ground stroke into the net on the fifth rally stroke. Thirty all.

Emma double faults. An early breakpoint for Rogers. Thirty forty.

Good serve down the T and Emma punishes the return with a forehand winner into Rogers' backhand court. Deuce.

A good return onto the baseline from Rogers causes Emma to hit a weak shot, which Rogers punishes with a forehand crosscourt winner. Second breakpoint.

Rogers hits the sixth rally stroke long. Second deuce.

Emma overhits the third rally stroke. Another breakpoint for Rogers.

Martina Navratilova: 'Both players overhitting on the baseline. That's adrenalin for you. They'll have to reel it in a little bit better.'

Emma hits a forehand crosscourt winner behind Rogers on the fifth rally stroke. Third deuce.

Emma hits the fifth rally stroke into the net, going for too much too soon. Breakpoint again for Rogers.

Martina Navratilova: 'You don't want to hit low percentage shots like that one was.'

A poor shot goes wide on the fifth rally stroke. Rogers wins the first game. Is Emma in trouble? Broken in her first game. Love-one.

***

They change ends. Great serve from Rogers. Fifteen love.

Rogers hits long off Emma's return. Fifteen all.

Both still nervous. Emma's talking to herself between points in this enormous stadium.

Rogers hits the net off Emma's return. Fifteen, thirty.

Good forehand winner for Rogers on the fifth rally stroke. Thirty all.

Good return from Emma and Rogers fires into the net. Breakback point for Emma. Thirty forty.

Emma's return loops into the net. Deuce.

Emma hits long on the fourth rally stroke. Advantage Rogers.

A good shot from Rogers has Emma hitting the fourth rally stroke on the run and it goes wide. Good hold for Rogers. Love-two.

***

Emma serving.

Rogers' return hits the net cord and drops over. Nothing is going right for Emma now. Love, fifteen.

Rogers' return is skied, and Emma runs towards the net with her racquet prepared for the smash, which beats the American. Fifteen all.

Martina Navratilova: 'Phew. Was holding my breath on that one. Swinging on a downward trajectory. It had to be timed perfectly.'

Double fault. Fifteen, thirty.

Emma overhits off Rogers' return. Fifteen forty. Danger.

Lovely serve deep into the forehand court, which Rogers only just reaches. Thirty forty.

Another great wide serve, and Rogers hits into the net. Deuce.

Good serve, and again the return hits the net. Advantage Emma.

Emma hits the fifth rally stroke into the net. Deuce again.

Mark Petchey: 'Lot of fast balls through the middle of the court from Rogers early on.'

Martina Navratilova: 'Rogers is not playing the same way she played against Ash Barty, looping the ball. This time she's going for a normal game, which is pretty much hit as hard as you can while still being as safe as possible, not necessarily changing the direction of the ball, but giving it a good wallop.'

Rogers hits the fourth rally stroke long. Game point for Emma.

Again, Rogers hits the net cord on the fourth rally stroke and the ball bounces off court. Emma's on the scoreboard. One-two.

***

Tim Henman, courtside: 'There's no doubt Emma is a little bit nervous out there. The footwork hasn't quite been as sharp, she hasn't quite got into a position, she's made a few unforced errors, and Rogers has definitely got the heavier weight of shot. That was a really good game to get under her belt and there's such a long way to go. No need to panic at this stage. I think she can find her rhythm at the back of the court and start to make an impression. Hopefully, that's going to change right now.'

The crowd is pouring into the stadium unsettling both players and having the umpire call for people to take any seat.

Rogers to serve.

An eleven-stroke rally with Emma not quite getting to a deep ground stroke. Fifteen love.

Emma only just gets to a deep shot by Rogers and the ball loops down into the backhand corner. Emma hits Rogers' reply super hard and the American hits into the net. Fifteen all.

Emma's return flies high and long. Thirty fifteen.

Emma's ground strokes are coming at Rogers much faster now and the American hits long on the fifth rally stroke. Thirty all.

Emma starting to hit much harder. They're matching each other point for point. Rogers hits into the net on the ninth rally stroke. Emma gets a breakpoint. Thirty forty.

Another long rally and Rogers hits the thirteenth rally stroke long. Emma's got the breakback. It is two-two.

***

Mark Petchey: 'You don't need to win all the points— just the right ones, and she's won a couple of big ones in those last two games.

Emma to serve.

Deep, wide serve and Rogers hits long across the court. Fifteen love.

Rogers's return loops over the net and Emma volleys it into Rogers' backhand service court. Thirty love.

Good play from Rogers who hits the sixth rally stroke into an open court. Thirty fifteen.

Martina Navratilova: 'Too good! Good body language from both players.'

Powerful rally from both women, but Rogers hits the fourteenth rally stroke long. Forty fifteen.

Deep, wide serve into Rogers' forehand and the return flies well long. Game to Emma and she's in front for the first time. She pumps her fist at her team box as she realises this could be a turning point. Three-two.

Mark Petchey: 'She rips off three straight games.'

***

Martina Navratilova: 'There is just so much different about this court. The size of it, the sight lines and then, you look up and there is the roof, or not, the wind is different, and the noise level here. What people don't really notice on TV, is you don't really hear the ball hitting the racquet that well, as it's so noisy. Just with no people here it's noisy, when they have air going and everything.'

Mark Petchey: 'Music to my ears, the amount of excuses I could have had if I had been out there!'

The empty seats are filling rapidly. Shelby Rogers is waiting for crowd movement to subside before serving.

Rogers tries to hit a backhand down the line on the fifth rally stroke, but it sails wide. Love fifteen.

Emma nods to some instruction she gives herself—keep calm, don't rush, play the high percentage strokes etc. no doubt.

A rushed forehand from Rogers on the fifth rally stroke sails wide. Love thirty.

Martina Navratilova: 'Of course, Shelby Rogers, because she's hitting the ball harder, it means when she misses, she misses big.'

Rogers puts Emma's return into the net. Three unforced errors gives three breakpoints to the Brit. Love forty.

Emma's return flies wide. Fifteen forty.

Good, deep shot from Rogers and Emma hits the crosscourt shot, on the fourth rally stroke, wide. Still breakpoint. Thirty forty.

Rogers hits Emma's return into the net. Emma breaks again. Now four games in a row. She shouts at her box and pumps her fist. Four games to two.

***

Mark Petchey: 'Spent a lot of time, has Raducanu, studying the likes of Halep [Emma's tennis idol] and Azarenka. Sometimes, young players think that these top players just ping balls to the line, instead of, actually the best quality of the very best players is repetitive shots to a certain area on the court. Big targets.'

Emma serving. Rogers punishes the second serve with a forehand down the line return. Love fifteen.

Good return and Emma hits the fifth rally stroke into the net. Love thirty.

Ace down the T. Fifteen thirty.

Mark Petchey: 'Equal fastest serve of the tournament there from Raducanu.' [110mph]

Rogers's return flies long. Thirty all.

Emma comes in and hits a forehand winner on the seventh stroke of the rally. Forty thirty.

Very wide ace. Game to Emma. Five-two.

Mark Petchey: 'How impressive is that run of five games for Emma Raducanu. Striding purposefully to her chair. It's Shelby Rogers who got out of the blocks very quickly with a couple of games, but Raducanu who has found herself within a game of this opening set. Martina, that is an impressive twenty minutes of play there from Emma.'

Martina Navratilova: 'You're not kidding. Love two down, again lost both games. She had game points lost them both, love forty down on her serve, held her nerve, held her serve and this game, also down love thirty, through no fault of her own and held again, so she's really playing the big points well, playing within herself, completely not nervous anymore at all. If the legs were not moving in the first couple of games, they're certainly moving now. She's defending well. She got herself out of trouble in a couple of longer rallies and kept the ball in play. I think that put some seed of doubt into Rogers' head and after that she wanted to go for more and she started missing more, so now Raducanu is in the driver's seat.'

***

New balls for Rogers. Brilliant return from Emma and Rogers hits long. Love fifteen.

Good serve down the T and Emma returns into the net. Fifteen all.

Emma whacks the fourth stroke of the rally and Rogers could do no more than fire it back into the net. Fifteen thirty.

Good deep crosscourt return from Emma's backhand into Rogers' backhand side and the American's backhand down the line is well wide. Two set points for Emma. Fifteen forty.

Mark Petchey: 'She had the distinct possibility, Shelby Rogers, of running away with this opening set, taking advantage of the fact that Emma Raducanu hadn't been out on this court before. It didn't happen when she had the chance to go up three love. The opportunity though for Raducanu to take the first set is here.'

Emma hits the return into the net. Thirty forty.

Martina Navratilova: 'It was there for the taking, at the time it doesn't seem like a big miss, but you never know. That was there for the taking.'

A massive forehand return from Emma hits the line as it passes Rogers. The teenager screams out at the success of taking the set by six games to two. She'd won six consecutive games.

***

Mark Petchey: 'Tim, that shot just there shows the depth of her self-belief, doesn't it?'

Tim Henman courtside: 'Yeah, absolutely. I mean it wasn't the ideal start going down two love, and you thought the nerves were really showing for Raducanu, but she showed such competitive spirit, composure just to work herself into this first set and now it's Rogers footwork that is looking a little bit heavy. Raducanu can stay in the rallies when she needs to, and when she gets the chance to pull the trigger, she's not shying, going for it, and that second serve return on setpoint was the perfect example.'

Mark Petchey: 'Obviously, you and Martina have played on this court numerous times over the course of your careers in these big sorts of occasions here. How impressed have you been in terms of Emma's attitude out there and demeanour?'

Tim Henman: 'Yeah, definitely. This is the biggest stadium in our sport. The dimensions outside the court do take getting used to. There's obviously a huge crowd in here so it's so important that Emma, you know, is able to focus on the job in hand, and when you're eighteen, never experienced this environment before, it is not easy to do, and having lost the first two games and to win the next six is mighty impressive. Great that she's got the first set under her belt. She needs to start all over again in this second set to maintain the momentum. Expect a reaction from Rogers. She has the experience.'

They come out for the second set with Emma to serve.

Big serve down the T, which Rogers can't return. Fifteen love.

Skied shot from Emma on the fifth rally stroke. Fifteen all.

Rogers can't hit the fourth rally stroke accurately. It hits the net. Thirty fifteen.

Emma puts the seventh rally stroke into the net, carelessly. Thirty all.

Rogers hits the sixth rally stroke into the net. Emma screams 'Come on!' as she whirls to return to the back of the court. Forty thirty.

A poor second serve gives Rogers the initiative on the return, but Emma's crosscourt shot is only hit back into the net. Game to Emma. Seven in a row. A set and a game up. One-love.

Martina Navratilova: 'I think she'll be expecting an easier shot after her killer return, and Emma was able to neutralise it really well with the forehand, get the ball low hard enough. Rogers went for too much and it was a good hold for Raducanu.'

***

Huge cheers as they change ends and Rogers is to serve.

Mark Petchey: 'The Americans are urging on one of their own.'

Emma's return is right on the line. Rogers gets it back, but Emma runs in and hits a forehand winner behind the American who expects it to go the other way. Love fifteen.

Emma's return is long. Fifteen all.

Rogers hits Emma's return into the net. Fifteen thirty.

A poor short return from Emma is fired into the net by Rogers. Two breakpoints. Fifteen forty.

A lot of crowd noise as Rogers prepares to serve to save the game.

Emma hits a forehand down the line on the sixth rally stroke and Rogers can only put it wide. Eight games on the bounce for the girl from Bromley. Two-love.

**

Mark Petchey: 'She hasn't got a plan at the moment.'

Martina Navratilova: 'Yeah, Raducanu is taking the time away from Shelby, she's still trying to hit her shots, but she's not in the position to do so. When she played Ash Barty, Shelby had more time to hit her shots, especially with the slice that Ash hits a lot. She had a lot more time to get set and pick her spots. Raducanu is giving it to her. She's bullying her around the court, nicely.'

Emma serving. Rogers wins the sixth rally stroke with a shot behind Emma. Love fifteen.

Emma misses a down the line shot on the fifth rally stroke. Love thirty.

Martina Navratilova: 'Not sure what happened there.'

Great wide serve, which Rogers can only return into the net. Fifteen thirty.

Good serve. Rogers returns wide. Thirty all.

Martina Navratilova: 'That was a good serve, but it wasn't a great serve. It was a really bad miss by Rogers. Not sure what happened there.'

Wide ace. Unreachable. Forty thirty.

Martina Navratilova: 'Great serve there, really taking the pace off the ball. Only 86 miles per hour, beautifully

90

short in the court, spinning away to the Mercedes sign on the side.'

Rogers hits the fourth rally stroke long. Nine games in a row, now. Three-love.

***

Mark Petchey: 'Again, it's another recovery from love, thirty.'

Martina Navratilova: 'She is just a superstar in the making. You don't want to put too much pressure on anybody, but you know when they're special. Like Nadal, Djokovic, Alcaraz, and Martina Hingis, yeah, they were born for it and the only really big concern is health. If the body is willing, I think everything else is there.'

Rogers to serve. Good return which Rogers fires into the net. Love fifteen.

Good crosscourt backhand return from Emma, and Rogers hits it wide. Love thirty.

This time, a good crosscourt forehand return and Rogers reply finds the net. Three breakpoints. Love forty.

Double fault. Emma has ten games in a row and now leads by four games to love.

***

Emma to serve. Rogers' return finds the net. Fifteen love.

Rogers overhits the sixth rally stroke. Thirty love.

Martina Navratilova: 'She cannot find the court, she cannot find the court! When a bad day happens, you know, somewhere else, but at this stage of the tournament on this particular stage—Arthur Ashe Stadium. It's eleven points in a row right now for Raducanu.'

Another return goes straight into the net. Forty love.

The stadium is exploding with noise and Emma stops to wait for quiet. The huge partisan crowd is behind the American, but there is a growing supportive noise for Emma too. Emma lets it wash over her and as the sound dies, she begins her cool, calm serve routine.

A huge cheer from the crowd as Emma hits Rogers' return into the net. Forty fifteen.

91

Mark Petchey: 'Well, it's a good return, but is it enough to mount any sort of recovery?'

Rogers' return is long. An eleventh game in a row for Emma. Five-love.

***

The players return to their seats. Billie Jean King appears on the stadium balcony and waves during the break, and the cheers ring out.

Mark Petchey: 'Emma has reeled off eleven games in a row for the second match in a row. A magnificent achievement.

'And the errors coming from the American and this incredible story that is developing with Raducanu looks as though it's going to continue into the last eight here at the U.S. Open. Eleven straight games.'

Martina Navratilova: 'I was worried for Raducanu for the first couple of games. She had game points in both games, lost them. Down love forty, two service breaks. An incredible achievement. Billie Jean King is soaking up the applause here.'

Emma comes out, with Rogers serving to save the match and her hope of reaching the quarterfinals.

Emma whacks an amazing forehand down the line return of serve. Total winner. Love fifteen.

A sixth rally stroke miss from Emma. Fifteen all.

Rogers comes into the net and plays a volley winner into Emma's forehand side on the fifth rally stroke. Thirty fifteen.

Huge cheers from the mainly partisan crowd.

Rogers hits the seventh rally stroke long. Thirty all.

Rogers runs in to a loopy return from Emma and smashes the volley to where Emma's standing. She gets her racquet to it, but the shot hits the net. More cheering from the crowd. Forty thirty.

Emma's return is long, and Rogers saves the bagel. The crowd cheer loudly. Five-one.

***

Emma steps out to serve for the match.

Rogers' loopy return eventually returns to Earth and is out. Fifteen love.

Amazing down the line return winner for Rogers. Fifteen all.

Emma hits Rogers' return long. Fifteen thirty.

Another winner from Rogers. A backhand down the line on the fourth rally point. Two breakpoints. Can she begin a fight back? Fifteen forty.

The return from Rogers hits the net cord and comes down on Emma's side. The teenager is on it in a flash and sends a shot down towards Rogers' forehand, which should then pass Emma, but she is quick enough to get her racquet to it and plays a dropshot.

Mark Petchey: 'How good is that?'

Martina Navratilova: 'Two hands on the racquet too! Gotta teach her a one handed backhand volley. Would be much easier.'

Rogers' return comes over the net, spinning and turning. Emma gets to it and plays a forehand winner behind the running American. Deuce.

Martina Navratilova: 'That's great stuff! That was a gnarly, gnarly return—had a funny spin on it from a mishit. She had to use turbo boosters there to get to that ball and still was able to control it well.'

Good serve into the backhand of Rogers. Emma runs in to the return and fires a backhand winning volley into Rogers' forehand corner. Match point for Emma.

Mark Petchey: 'Perfection personified and delivered by Emma Raducanu.'

Emma hits Rogers' return into the net cord and bounces wide. Second deuce.

Emma puffs out her cheeks and steadies herself to serve.

Good serve and Rogers returns into the net. Second match point.

She shakes her fist, nods for a ball and starts her serve routine.

Emma hits Rogers' return long. Third deuce.

Rogers hits an amazing forehand crosscourt winner. Advantage to the American.

Emma hits the American's return back to the same corner. Rogers skies the shot, Emma runs in and hits a forehand volley winner behind the running opponent. Fourth deuce.

Emma runs in on Rogers' return and hits a forehand crosscourt winner. Third match point.

Rogers hits an eminently hittable return, but Emma strikes early, and it flies wide, showing that she does have some nerves. Fifth deuce.

Another one-two for Emma, finishing with a forehand into the left court. She screams 'Come on!' at the Arthur Ashe Stadium in general. Fourth match point.

Rogers hits the second serve return into the net. Emma drops her racquet and bends double, drops to her knees momentarily, then rises, both laughing, smiling and hiding her mouth at delight for what she has achieved. She's won the match on the biggest tennis arena in the world, six two, six one, and is in the quarterfinals of the U.S. Open.

***

Mark Petchey: 'She despatches Shelby Rogers, the conqueror of Ash Barty in the previous round, losing just three games.'

A disappointed Shelby Rogers, loved by the crowd, is signing autographs and posing for selfies as she makes her way towards the exit.

Being in the Arthur Ashe Stadium, there is an immediate interview with Emma on the court.

Rennae Stubbs: 'Congratulations on your first major quarterfinal.'

Huge cheers ring out and Emma waves at the crowd, beaming and smiling in embarrassment and disbelief.

Rennae Stubbs: 'We saw you play your first Wimbledon a couple of months ago, got through to the second week, how do you compare what it feels like here in New York to get to the second week *and* one round further?'

Emma: 'Thank you. It feels absolutely amazing to play in front of all of you, and Shelby is a great opponent. She's done so well here in the U.S. Open, and she's had a great week, so I knew it was going to be a tough match, but I'm so happy to have managed to come through and overcome some of the nerves at the beginning.'

Rennae Stubbs: 'Yesterday, you got to watch two eighteen-year-olds, Leylah today turned nineteen. They won their matches. How is that inspiring you as you play the next day to try to equal their round?'

Emma: 'I mean, it definitely plays a part in motivation, like I wanted to join them as well, but everyone's on their own trajectory and I'm just so happy to have been able to focus on my game, and into the quarter finals.'

Again, a burst of applause and cheering, which makes Emma almost cringe, but laughing at the unreality, as she looks around to take it all in.

Rennae Stubbs: 'There is a lot of tennis history trying to be written here at the 2021 U. S. Open. Behind my left shoulder in the front row of the president's box is Virginia Wade, the winner of this first Open Championship in 1968,' the interviewer is interrupted by a cacophony of sound as Virginia Wade waves towards the camera. Emma seeks out the British tennis icon in the box. Rennae Stubbs struggles to continue over the noise, 'the winner of Wimbledon in 1977, and you just finished your, I don't know, A-levels or whatever it's called in Great Britain, what do you know about tennis history and do you wanna say hi to Virginia Wade?'

Emma shouts over the crowd noise: 'Thank you so much for watching my match. I really appreciate it, and you're an absolute legend, so I'm really honoured to have had you here, and, yeah, I'm gonna just try and do my best each round and let's see how far it goes.' Emma is laughing and smiling as the applause rings out around her.

Rennae Stubbs: 'In your first major quarterfinal, Belinda Bencic who won Olympic gold at Tokyo. Do you want to give us a little bit of a preview of how you expect that match, or what you need to do to prepare best for that quarterfinal?'

Emma: 'Of course, I mean, Belinda is a great player who is in great form, so I know I'm gonna have to bring *it* on Wednesday. It's just gonna be who can dictate and I'm just not really thinking about tennis right now, but I'll leave that for tomorrow.' She laughs again, unable to believe the adoration that is pouring from the stands.

Rennae Stubbs: 'I'll let you have the last word. Do you want to say anything else to this crowd today?'

Emma: 'I mean, thank you so much for watching and all the support. I still love playing in front of you all.' She was interrupted by cheers and applause. 'So, all my matches here in New York I've received unbelievable support and you made me feel so at home and welcome. I'm really, really grateful.'

Rennae Stubbs: 'Thank you very much, Emma, and all the best in the quarterfinal.'

Back to the studio and Catherine Whitaker: 'What a moment, what a player, what a young woman, we have on our hands in Emma Raducanu. The youngest British quarter finalist at the U.S. Open in sixty-two years, since Christine Truman in 1955. She's the youngest [Brit] at any slam since Sue Barker at the Australian Open in 1975. What incredible company to be in. She's been watched today in the Arthur Ashe Stadium by Virginia Wade, Billie Jean King, and Martina Navratilova. These are just incredible moments. We may or may not have something in our eyes watching these moments from Raducanu, so let's let Tim take the spotlight for a minute. Tim, you had the best seat in the house for what was not a very long match in the end, but how does it feel to have witnessed something so special up close.'

Tim Henman: 'Catherine, it was so special out here to see Raducanu get off to that nervous start down two love, you know, you feel for her. It takes a lot of courage, a lot of guts to dig your heels in and fight your way out of that. I just didn't expect her to respond in that fashion, and to then win the next six games and win the first set six two. Then to maintain the momentum in the early part of the second set, I mean, it really is an incredible performance. Even up six two, five one, it's not easy to finish off these big matches. I was really impressed with the way she kept her composure, took her time, and to beat Shelby Rogers six two, six one, who obviously beat Ash Barty, the world number one, in the previous round, is an incredible result.'

Catherine Whitaker: 'We will enjoy the moment, Tim, and will try not to get carried away, but also when are we allowed to think the unthinkable?'

Tim Henman: 'I'm having difficulty hearing you over the crowd noise. It's, you know, we just gotta go one match at a time. I mean, she's so inexperienced. We gotta reflect on her ranking. There's no good thinking about semi-finals and finals, she's got to play the Olympic champion, and this is a significant step up in form. As well as Raducanu played today, Rogers didn't pose so many threats, her movement wasn't as good, but Bencic is a different class. There's no doubt that Bencic is the clear favourite for that match, so Raducanu's gotta prepare as best she can and get ready for that one.'

Greg Rusedski: 'I agree with Tim, because we have finally seen a player who we believe can possibly, one day, win slams in the women's game, so for me it's a big moment.'

Martina Navratilova, in the commentary booth: 'Just because Virginia Wade was here that makes it even more special. I did not know she was there, and Emma probably didn't know either. It's a good thing she didn't. What a way of coming out in New York City by getting this far, in this tournament, and then beating an American on Arthur Ashe court in this fashion, keeping her head about her as well as she did. You know, she might have done well in the A-levels but she's gotten an A in tennis psychology as well, because she really knows what she's doing out there, in every aspect of the game, and the mental one. That's the one that takes the longest to get and she's already there.'

Mark Petchey in the commentary booth: 'Yes, I agree with you, Martina. The other thing is that Emma, for me, didn't play her best tennis today and she found a way to stay calm and composed, and you kind of felt, after she got over that two love game, and managed to hold, she went from strength to strength and showed so much mental fortitude.'

Catherine Whitaker in the studio: 'Yeah, we had Billie Jean King watching from courtside. You champions, Martina, you know the qualities when you see them, right? Is there anything in particular about Emma that tells you she's got it?'

Martina Navratilova: 'Well everything, everything that she's been doing really. The way she plays, the technique is impeccable, her tennis IQ is extremely high, and the emotional level-headedness that she has—that's really hard to come by, so she's really the whole package. But as Tim says, you don't want to think winning right now. It's Belinda Bencic next, is all that matters at the moment.'

Catherine Whitaker, 'Yeah, Belinda Bencic, Mark, a very very different test. Is it an achievable test for Emma Raducanu at this stage?'

Mark Petchey: 'I think it's achievable if she can keep it close. Yeah, I think that Belinda's obviously got a lot of confidence right now off the back of the Olympics. Sometimes, this year, she's been a little bit up and down with her performances. She's a very flat hitter of the ball. If she is nervous, she can also make an awful lot of errors. There can be some frailty around the second serve, but you only tend to see that if the scoreboard's close against these great players. Obviously, having overcome so many of those sorts of issues at the Olympics, it's kind of a good time for Belinda to take on Emma when she's feeling as confident as that, but look, everything is possible at the end of the day, and with the way that Emma's playing and competing and moving in particular, she's got a realistic shot against anybody out there.'

Martina Navratilova: 'Yeah, Bencic was a bit hot and cold today. Swaitek didn't play her best tennis and still should have won the first set. Bencic just started losing it a little bit and if she gets streaky against Emma, she will pay the price.'

8 Belinda Bencic—U.S. Open Quarterfinal

Belinda Bencic, world number twelve from Switzerland, five feet nine inches tall, twenty-four years old, Olympic Champion at the 2020 Tokyo Olympics (held in 2021 owing to Covid)[xv]. She is the first top twenty player who Emma has faced.

Before the quarterfinal, tennis presenter, Catherine Whitaker, said, 'I'm having visions of a Fernandez, Raducanu final.' A rather remarkable insight… or just luck?

Surely, it could not be possible, but pundits were beginning to discuss the possibility of the teenage Brit going all the way.

Again, the venue was the world's biggest tennis stadium, the Arthur Ashe court at the Billie Jean King Tennis Center in Flushing Meadows, New York.

Emma arrived on court in her signature, red and blue NY Slam outfit, with the same yellow sun visor, smiling and waving at the growing crowd. She has developed a cold sore on her upper lip, but it doesn't detract from that charming, natural smile.

In a later press conference, Emma was asked about her outfit and whether it was superstition that she kept to the same skirt and top. She was quick to point out that it wasn't the same and she laughed that she had more than one. She liked red, and as it had served her well so far, she didn't want to tempt fate by changing it. If truth be told, she wore shorts rather than a skirt with the same top in the first round of qualifying.

Belinda Bencic wore a yellow tennis dress with navy insets to the sides and navy shoes. She quickly tied her ponytail up into a topknot at her seat and wore a blue visor.

Emma carried her extra-long, Wilson 100 Steam racquet painted as a Blade, and Bencic was using a Vonex.

Catherine Whitaker[xvi], in the studio, asked the GB team captain how Emma would be feeling as she walked onto the court.

Anne Keothavong: 'Well, I'm sure there will be a combination of nerves and excitement. It's a big moment, but you know, I don't think she can be any better prepared than she is for this moment. She's had a lot of people, good people around her who I'm sure have given other words of wisdom that she needs to hear, but no, just go out there and give it your best shot.'

Annabel Croft: 'I guess she has to just keep doing exactly the routines that she's had throughout the seven matches. We have to remember those three matches in qualies, and then the four in the main draw, and she's got into a routine. She's on a roll and you just keep that routine going. Her team will have prepared her for every eventuality, so she'll have a lot of little things going through her head for what might or might not happen, but she always comes out and appears to play with freedom, with abandon, she comes out of the blocks very quickly and she's taken her game to all opponents, and I think she'll do exactly the same today.'

The commentators are Mary Joe Fernandez and Mark Petchey. Catherine asked Mary Joe how she thought Emma would be feeling.

Mary Joe Fernandez: 'Well, I think she will definitely be nervous, but nerves aren't always a bad thing. You want to have that tension, you need to really feel ready, and I think when you're nervous you know that the anticipation is there, and it's a question of loosening up in the warm-up, hitting out, hitting as hard as you can to just relax a little bit, but the fact that she played a couple of days ago against Shelby Rogers, she was nervous at the start. I think that's gonna help her today against Bencic, who has not played on Ashe for two years, when she reached the semis.'

Mark Petchey: 'I think Mary Joe makes a great point. It is a little quicker out on Ashe compared to the outside courts. Emma felt that after her match against Shelby, and so, obviously that's a huge advantage for her going in today. She understands what she is going to face, she knows what Bencic does in terms of the flat hit, and she realises how the surface is going to come through lower, so she's going to sink, she's going to use her legs a little bit more. I think it's those little nuances such as the shade and the sun today that all the players, are going to have to get used to and deal with.'

Mary Joe Fernandez: 'Emma's become the darling of America as well, I mean, she is delightful. Her interviews are just really sweet. She comes off as just such a mature young woman already, with such a good head on her shoulders, so the American crowd has totally embraced Emma.'

The match begins.

Emma's second serve is returned and Emma hits wide. Love fifteen.

On the seventh rally stroke, Emma hits wide. Love thirty.

Deep return from Bencic and Emma hits into the net. Three breakpoints early on. Not good for the Brit. Love forty.

Mary Joe Fernandez: 'The jitterbugs are there, early on. She experienced this a couple of days ago against Shelby Rogers.'

Amazing second serve ace down the T. Fifteen forty.

Emma hits the seventh rally stroke into the net. Break for Bencic. Love-one.

***

Mark Petchey: 'Bencic settling nicely, not to be unexpected, full of confidence after Tokyo, but also just a huge amount of experience as well.'

They change ends. The shadow splits the court in half and Emma is now receiving in the sunshine.

Emma's return is long. Fifteen love.

On the eighth rally stroke, Emma hits a forehand winner down the line. Fifteen all.

Trying to go for too much on the return, Emma's shot hits the net. Thirty fifteen.

Emma hits the sixth rally stroke into the net. Forty fifteen.

Bencic's ground strokes are hard, but Emma is returning them with interest. Unfortunately, her shot on the sixth rally stroke goes into the net and Bencic is two up. Love-two.

***

Mark Petchey: 'Solid opening [service] game there from Bencic. It's going to be a balancing act at the start of this match as Raducanu tries to find out what works, Mary Joe.'

Mary Joe Fernandez: 'Definitely, I mean that was a confidence building game from Bencic. Didn't make a first serve and was still able to win it quite comfortably. An important game, right now, for Raducanu to settle in—to feel that she really belongs on this stage.'

Emma serving. Good one-two for Emma. Bencic runs crosscourt on the return, but Emma came in and fired a forehand winner behind the Swiss player. Fifteen love.

Bencic hits the return long. Thirty love.

It's clear that Emma is stressed. Breathing deeply.

Bencic's forehand return from Emma's serve down the T is short. The Brit comes in and hits a crosscourt backhand winner, which lands on the line. Forty love.

Emma coming in too quickly off Bencic's return allows the Swiss player to pass her down the line. Forty fifteen.

Another Bencic backhand winner, this time crosscourt, on the fourth rally stroke. Forty thirty.

Mary Joe Fernandez: 'Good tennis from Bencic. She is timing the return off the second serve, leaning in, gets Emma on the back foot. She's seeing the ball well.'

Bencic tries to play a down the line winning return but the shot goes wide. Emma's game, she's on the scoreboard. One-two.

Mark Petchey: 'That was a big point.'

***

After the break. Bencic serving. The crowd is pouring into the stadium and the umpire is scolding them for not sitting down more quickly. 'The players are waiting,' he shouts.

Mark Petchey: 'Bencic, of course, didn't travel last summer due to the covid restrictions, but if she wins today, she's back in the world's top ten. [She had reached number four in the past] and is the highest ranked opponent Emma has played, and she is one of the elite.'

The crowd is still flooding into the Arthur Ashe Stadium.

The umpire is telling people to take any seat to allow the match to continue.

Emma hits the fourth rally stroke into the net. Fifteen love.

Bencic's first serve is in the net. Someone in the crowd breaks the silence with, 'Come on, Emma!'

Second serve, good return, but Emma hits the fourth rally stroke wide, pushing too much. Thirty love.

Mary Joe Fernandez: 'Pressing a little bit too much early on Raducanu, overplaying. I think she feels the need to be aggressive coz she knows Bencic will take over if not.'

Emma's short return is run to by Bencic who just manages to play a shot. Emma again hits wide, trying to make the winner. Missed opportunity. Forty love.

Good, deep serve. Emma's backhand return is skied, and Bencic hits a good swing volley into the open court. One-three.

***

Emma to serve.

Deep serve into Bencic's forehand. The return flies long. Fifteen love.

Ace for Emma down the T. Thirty love.

Mary Joe Fernandez: 'I wonder if changing the pace and hitting some higher shots, loopier balls, as long as they're still fairly deep into the court, would be a good thing.'

Mark Petchey: 'One hundred percent. Andrew Richardson had her doing that this morning, as well as lots of high balls down the line off the floor. Not easy when it's coming in fast and low. She had a lot of sliced backhands as well, trying to keep the ball or anything to make the net much more of an obstacle for Bencic, is huge.'

There is a shout for 'Emma!' from the crowd after Emma's shot off Bencic's return. It clearly distracted the Swiss player and she hit long. Forty love.

The umpire scolds the crowd, 'Please do not shout out during play. Thank you very much.'

Bencic hits the sixth stroke of the rally long. Emma wins the game to love. Still only a single break of serve. Two-three.

Mary Joe Fernandez: 'That is the best game we've seen from Raducanu. Now she's got to get involved in Bencic's service games. She's in the match now and feeling a little better. Starting to serve a bit better too.'

***

Bencic to serve. Emma hits a crosscourt forehand return. Bencic sends it back to Emma's forehand corner and the Brit hits another forehand down the line. Total winner. Love fifteen.

Emma's return off a second serve finds the net. Fifteen all.

Emma is talking to herself and waving her arm to practice what she should have done to the return.

Emma's return is powerful and deep. Bencic hits long. Fifteen thirty.

Good serve. The return is down the middle and Bencic punishes it with a backhand crosscourt winner. Thirty all.

Good, powerful ground strokes from both players, but on the eleventh rally stroke, Bencic hits long. Breakpoint. Thirty forty.

Mary Joe Fernandez: 'Much better ball striking by Raducanu, extending the rally and staying shot for shot with Bencic.'

The third stroke of the rally reaches Emma, and her shot comes off the frame into the crowd, causing the usual cheers as spectators try to catch the ball. Deuce.

Bencic double faults. Breakpoint number two.

Great serve down the T, but Emma's return sends it back with interest and Bencic hits into the net. The breakback is complete. Three games all.

***

Emma to serve.

On the fifth rally stroke, Emma plays a lob over the advancing Bencic, but it lands a fraction long. Love fifteen.

Emma's shot on the ninth rally stroke is short, Bencic punishes it, and Emma's next backhand is overhit. Love thirty.

A deep second serve into Bencic's forehand just clips the line and the Swiss player's return can do no more than find the net. Fifteen thirty.

Another good second serve and Bencic mistimes the return into the net. Thirty all.

Good serve, a short return, and Emma hits a glorious, backhand crosscourt winner beyond the scrambling Bencic. Forty thirty.

Mary Joe Fernandez: 'Really well done by Raducanu. It's a good first serve again into the forehand of Bencic who mishits the return a little bit, and then she stays low, gets that left hand to do a lot of the work to get the angle.'

Bencic hits the sixth rally stroke into the net. A good hold. Finally, Emma's in front. Raducanu is pumping her fist and shouting to the crowd as she marches purposefully to her seat. Four games to three.
***

Mark Petchey, speaking during the break: 'Raducanu revelling in the atmosphere, finally in front for the first time in this quarterfinal. Terrific couple of games for her and that will have Bencic wondering.'

The umpire calls for new balls.

Mary Joe Fernandez: 'That was a good effort from love thirty, consolidating the break. Bencic has a few unforced errors in the last couple of games. She's starting to feel the pressure of what Raducanu can do.'

Mark continues: 'Twenty-five wins over top ten players for Bencic. She is pure class when she plays well. She has four wins over world number ones. Three against Osaka, one against Serena in that amazing run through as a teenager in Toronto in 2015. That heralded her arrival, but she's got wins over Kerber, Halep, Kvitova, Wozniacki, Venus Williams, Ivanovic when she was at the top, Garcia, Svitolina, the list goes on. This is a huge test today for Raducanu.'

Bencic serving. She has Emma running back and forth along the baseline, but she reaches every ball. Suddenly Bencic finds herself pinned to the forehand end of her baseline and Emma strikes a backhand down the line winner on the twelfth rally stroke to take the point. Emma's pumping her fist at the crowd. Love fifteen.

Mary Joe Fernandez: 'That's excellent tennis. Wonderful play by Raducanu, changing the pattern of the point, going down the line with the backhand. This is what changed it, and then she's in control. I love that she is trying to change things up and not allowing Bencic to get into her comfort zone of being the only one to redirect the ball.'

Brilliant backhand crosscourt from Bencic off Emma's return. Fifteen all.

This time a forehand down the line winner off the return, which Emma can't get back. Thirty fifteen.

Emma's return off the second serve sees Bencic hit into the net. Thirty all.

Emma's nodding and talking to herself on the baseline, jumping up and down. Waiting for Bencic to get ready to serve.

Bencic double faults, giving Emma a breakpoint. Thirty forty.

A good serve forces Emma to return into the net. Deuce.

Twenty strokes in the rally, and the winner is a forehand down the line, which leaves Bencic stranded in the forehand side of her court. A second breakpoint.

Mark Petchey: 'Unbelievable!'

Mary Joe Fernandez: 'Fantastic point by both players. Bencic is doing a great job in defence. She hit a slice in the middle of this rally to get back in the point but look at this outright winner [watching the point replay] from Raducanu. She's getting the depth, she's getting the angles and when she sees the opening to go down the line, she's measuring it beautifully.'

Mark Petchey: 'Stunning point. Another breakpoint.'

Emma's return only just clears the net. Bencic runs in to hit it back and Emma piles another winner past the Swiss player. Four games in a row. Just one game away from the set. Five games to three.

Mark Petchey: 'Well, she got fortunate, but she capitalised on it. Just wow!'

Mary Joe Fernandez: 'Impressive, she has totally turned the tables in this first set on Belinda Bencic, from three one down, has been a much better player more consistent and more aggressive.'

***

Emma's preparing to serve for the set.

Mark Petchey: 'I don't know what her heart rate is right now, but mine's pretty high.'

Ace for Emma down the T. Fifteen love.

Mary Joe Fernandez: 'It's always exciting when you see a teenager perform at such a high level, consistently, on the biggest stage.'

Bencic returns an extremely deep wide serve, but Emma fails to control the down the line shot, and it goes wide. Fifteen all.

Mary Joe Fernandez: 'We must remind everyone that this is Emma's first U.S. Open.'

Mark Petchey: 'I've got sweaters which are older than Emma!'

Terrific deep wide serve into Bencic's forehand and Emma runs in to a short return to finish the point with a forehand drive behind the Swiss woman. Thirty fifteen.

Mary Joe Fernandez: 'Beautiful, clever. Raducanu uses that wide serve again, but this time goes behind Bencic on the short one.'

Emma hits deep into Bencic's backhand on the third point of the rally. The ball comes back crosscourt, and the Brit is there to play a backhand winner down the line. The crowd explodes with cheers. Two set points for the teenager. Forty fifteen.

Good first serve. Bencic's return is long. Game and first set to Emma. Huge applause from the crowd. Six-three.

***

Mark Petchey in the commentary box: 'A standard of tennis that was just bewitching. Tim, sitting courtside watching that after the start that she had in her first ever quarterfinal of a major, is just outstanding.'

Tim Henman, courtside: 'It is. There's technical battles out there, there's physical battles out there, but there was an enormous mental battle early doors there for Emma. It's her resilience, she shows such maturity, she doesn't panic. Bencic didn't miss a shot for the first two and half games. If you're talking about the ideal way to start against the young pretender, that's it. She didn't give her anything, but there was no panic from Raducanu, she settled herself. That was a big service game to hold two one and then she's just gone from strength to strength, and you know, from Bencic being very settled early on, Raducanu has certainly rocked the boat, so it's a great first set to get under her belt, but as we all know, there is a long, long way to go.'

Bencic has left the court at the set break. Emma has won a remarkable five consecutive games.

When Bencic returns, she is to serve.

Bencic hits the seventh rally stroke into the net. Love fifteen.

Emma's return long. Fifteen all.

Bencic's third double fault, both into the net. Fifteen thirty.

Good rally. Once again, Emma has Bencic running, but the Swiss manages a great passing shot on the eleventh rally stroke as Emma had come in to finish her off. Thirty all.

Mary Joe Fernandez: 'Once again, Bencic anticipating the approach from Raducanu, doesn't move. Emma thought she was clearly going to go to the open court, but she doesn't, and strikes a pass really well.'

109

Good one-two for Bencic, hitting behind Emma. Forty thirty.

Good wide serve into Emma's backhand and the return finds the net. Important hold for Bencic. Love-one.

***

Emma is serving.

Bencic hits into the net on the eighth stroke of the rally. Fifteen love.

On the fifth rally stroke, Emma's shot down the line misses by millimetres. Fifteen all.

Emma long again on the ninth stroke of the rally, overhitting the shot. Fifteen thirty.

Mary Joe Fernandez: 'Bencic with the change of pace, throwing up a few higher balls. Don't see her do that too often, so that's a sign she's trying to problem solve.'

Unforced error from Emma, hitting into the net on the seventh rally stroke. Breakpoint for Bencic. Emma's shaking her head. Fifteen forty.

Mark Petchey: 'The tables are turning at the start of the second [set].'

Unflustered, Emma begins her service routine.

Great backhand down the line off Bencic's return to save the first breakpoint. Thirty forty.

Emma hits the forehand corner of Bencic's court on the third rally stroke, and when the ball comes back, she hits a terrific forehand down the line to win the point. Deuce.

Beautiful backhand return down the line from Bencic, taking advantage of the second serve. Breakpoint again.

Bencic's return into the net. Deuce.

Wide serve from Emma, then she hits Bencic's return behind her to get to advantage.

Bencic hits long on the fourth rally stroke and waves her arms in the air in frustration. One game all.

***

What can Bencic do on her serve?

Emma blows on each hand as she waits for Bencic to prepare.

Emma hits wide on the fourth rally stroke. Fifteen love.

Unreturnable serve. Thirty love.

Another powerful serve, this time down the T. Emma gets to it, but can only hit into the net. Forty love.

Deep, wide serve and Emma's return is into the net. Good serving from Bencic to win the game to love. One-two.

**

Emma's out early, before the call of 'time', testing the sun's position, ready to serve.

Unreturnable 110mph first serve, Emma's equal fastest of the tournament. Fifteen love.

Bencic hits the fourth stroke of the rally long. Thirty love.

Sixth stroke backhand crosscourt winner from Bencic. Thirty fifteen.

Another good winner for the Olympic champion, forehand behind Emma on the eighth rally stroke. Thirty all.

Fourth ace from Emma landed on the side line, out wide, and Bencic couldn't get close to it. Forty thirty,

Mary Joe Fernandez: 'Barely touched the line to give her fourth ace on it. Huge point.

Mark Petchey: 'Three millimetres in. Already has four aces in the match, but just had nine for the entire tournament in the main draw coming into this.

Bencic's return flies long. Two games all.

**

Bencic serves.

Emma stretches to reach a good serve, but the return is good enough to force Bencic to play into the net. Love fifteen.

The tenth rally stroke sees Emma hit a great crosscourt shot, having already had Bencic on the run. The Swiss player reaches it, but fires into the net. Love thirty.

This time, Bencic has Emma running, and on the seventh rally stroke, hits a backhand winner Emma can't reach. Fifteen thirty.

Mary Joe Fernandez: 'Oh, beautiful. That was a big point, love thirty. Bencic held her nerve. Emma did a good job to make her hit a few extra shots here, but it was Bencic dictating deep into the court. That's her favourite shot, the backhand. She'll run around her forehand many times to hit this one. Much more stable.'

Second serve and what a forehand return, stranding the server on the baseline. Emma has two more breakpoints. Fifteen forty.

Bencic double faults and Emma has the break. Three-two.

***

Mark Petchey: 'Wow! It continues. The fairy tale here in New York for Emma Raducanu. She is a set and a break up in her first ever major quarterfinal. Going from strength to strength. Mary Joe, we Brits, we're becoming believers.'

Mary Joe Fernandez: 'You should be. Emma Raducanu is the real deal.'

Mark Petchey: 'In a city which never sleeps, Emma Raducanu is putting her name up in lights.'

Emma serving. Bencic hits the sixth rally stroke, but it clips the net. Emma is on it in a flash, scrambles to change shot and plays a winning backhand into the open court. Fifteen love.

Bencic is looking angry, hands on hips, then slaps her thigh in frustration as she prepares to receive another serve from the teenager.

Ace down the T. Thirty love.

Bencic's return flies a fraction long. Bencic looks despondent, disbelieving. Talking to the world and looking up at the sky or is it just at the big screen which is showing the Hawkeye image of the miss. Forty love.

As if venting her anger on Emma, Bencic punishes the second serve with a massive return. Forty fifteen.

Bencic is gesticulating towards her team. She's known to get a little flaky under pressure.

On the fifth stroke of the rally, Emma hits another powerful Bencic shot into the net. Forty thirty.

Mary Joe Fernandez: 'You have to expect Bencic to go for a little bit more. When you feel like your back's against the wall you go for bigger shots, so Raducanu has to hold her off right here, right now!'

Bencic hits a vicious return, which would have been a winner, but for clipping the net cord and flying slightly long. Four games to two.

Mark Petchey: 'The deflection of the net was all that was necessary to take it out.'

***

The shadow on the court now only covers one side beyond the service line. Bencic prepares to serve from the sunshine end.

Going for too much, Bencic hits the fifth rally stroke wide and is gesturing towards her team box in frustration. Love fifteen.

Mary Joe Fernandez: 'Look at that stat. Zero unforced errors for Emma in this second set. [Eight for Bencic.]'

Emma struggles to hit a return and it flies long. Fifteen all.

Emma can't reach the next serve other than to deflect it. Thirty fifteen.

Bencic tries to do too much off a good length return and hits wide. Thirty all.

Mark Petchey: 'That just shows how confused Bencic is right now.'

Bencic double faults, the second one overhit. She turns and looks up to the sky. A breakpoint for Emma. Thirty forty.

On the seventh stroke, a desperate, lunging passing shot from Bencic saves the day, making Emma look at her team and smile. Deuce.

Mary Joe Fernandez: 'Emma Raducanu did a great job with this passing shot, getting it low, making Bencic hit the extra pass. She'll remember that point if Bencic finds a way to get herself back in this.'

On the fifth rally stroke, a dropshot from Bencic and Emma sprints to it, but just too late. Game point to the Swiss player.

Mary Joe Fernandez: 'Great feel there. The drop volley winner.'

Emma skies the fourth rally stroke and Bencic rushes in to play a winner into the open court. Four-three.

***

Mark Petchey: 'The Olympic gold medallist shows her class.'

Mary Joe Fernandez: 'That was an enormous hold for Bencic. Maybe, we'll see her venture forward a little bit more these next couple of games. Did really well at the net.'

Mark Petchey: 'Bencic just played beautifully. It was the sort of moment in a match that, if your mind can't stay in the present, you can start lingering on the opportunity that was there.'

Emma to serve.

Bencic makes a good return off Emma's serve. Emma hits it into the net. Love fifteen.

Emma double faults. Love thirty.

Mark Petchey: 'Raducanu, who's weathered a few storms in this match is going to need to do so again.'

Bencic hits the return well long. Fifteen thirty.

Mary Joe Fernandez: 'Raducanu took the pace off that first serve. Caught Bencic off guard.'

The fourth rally stroke goes long for Bencic. Bencic smashes her racquet into the court, then examines it, checking for damage. Thirty all.

Mary Joe Fernandez: 'She'll take that gift as well.'

Bencic returns into the net. Forty thirty.

Mark Petchey: 'Every player is different, but Bencic, we know, when she gets a little nervous, she swings harder. She swings big anyway and it's tough to catch up to the ball and connect with it properly. Point for five three in the second.'

Another return into the net and Emma is ahead by five games to three. One game from the semi-finals. Five-three.

***

Bencic serving. She seems to have the Brit in trouble, but then overhits the seventh rally stroke. It's long. Love fifteen.

Mark Petchey: 'Superb tenacity from Raducanu.'

Bencic has Emma running again and wins the ninth rally stroke. Fifteen all.

Good return off a second serve and Bencic hits the fifth shot long. Fifteen thirty.

Great serve out wide. Thirty all.

Emma goes for too much on her return and it hits the net. Forty thirty.

Mary Joe Fernandez: 'I don't mind the miss. Her intentions were right to be aggressive.'

Ace down the T for Bencic. Emma's going to have to serve for the match. Five-four.

***

Mark Petchey: 'Bencic gives herself one final chance to recover the elusive break in this second set, to keep her hopes alive of a second visit to the semi-finals at the U.S. Open. The biggest game of Emma Raducanu's life is coming up.'

Mary Joe Fernandez: 'You almost have to play some mind games with yourself, maybe pretend you're down five four instead of up five four, but she's gotta control what's in her control. First serves, first strikes when she has time do what she's been doing well, changing the direction of the ball. She's gotta go one point at a time.'

During the break, Emma is trying to stay cool, playing the air conditioning over her face and body. She's out on the court before the umpire calls 'time'. It's known that Bencic doesn't like being rushed between points.

Going for a winner, Emma hits into the net on the thirteenth rally stroke. Love fifteen.

Emma double faults. Love thirty. Danger for the Brit.

Bencic's return goes long. Fifteen thirty.

Slice return from Bencic is poor and Emma hits the forehand winner into Bencic's backhand side. Thirty all.

Emma shouts 'Come on!' to the world at large.

Magnificent, pinpoint accurate wide serve for another ace. Match point for Emma.

Someone in the crowd shouts her name and she stops her serve and re-prepares.

On the seventh rally stroke, Emma sends Bencic the wrong way and the Swiss player's shot hits the net. Game set and match to Emma Raducanu, six three, six four. She's in the semi-final!

***

Emma has dropped her racquet and is smiling and laughing and waving at the cheering crowd in disbelief. She holds her head in embarrassment and shock, gradually spinning around to take in all the adoration from the huge audience, then covering her face to hide her delight.

Mark Petchey: 'Emma Raducanu is fast becoming the queen of Queens, through to the last four here at the U.S. Open. It's not midnight yet in New York and the Cinderella story continues.'

Mary Joe Fernandez: 'It sure does. What an amazing performance. She has to be absolutely thrilled. She faced adversity in some of those service games, love thirty, and she handled the occasion beautifully, kept calm, made good decisions. Really played the best match—in my opinion—of the tournament. Outstanding.'

Rennae Stubbs steps up for the on court, interview. Emma is still in fits of smiling laughter. 'Well, ladies and gentlemen, you're seeing history. The first time ever in the history of the U.S. Open, a semi-finalist from the qualifying! Emma Raducanu, what a moment. Emma, I know you're taking all of this in, you're looking around you, can't believe what's happened. At the beginning of this match, explain, you looked a little bit nervous, it's a big moment, but for you, how did you turn it around after the start?'

Emma can't stop laughing and smiling, but finally composes herself: 'Of course, I mean, playing Belinda, she's such a great opponent and she's in unbelievable form. Her ball speed definitely caught me off guard, because she hits the ball so hard. I had to try and adjust and adapt, and it was a really tough match for me and I'm just so, so happy to have come through and thank you so much for all of your support today.'

Rennae has to wait for the deafening applause to die down before continuing: 'Emma, I don't think people understand. You've come through qualifying, now you've won this many matches in the main draw, physically and emotionally and mentally, how are you doing this?'

Emma laughs and smiles and tries to compose herself. She looks towards her team's box: 'I've got an absolutely amazing team here with me. Everyone over there, well they're keeping me in one piece, and I also have a team back home that we've been staying in contact, but they couldn't be here [Covid 19 pandemic], but I'm sure they're watching... I hope.'

More cheers and applause and Emma laughs at what she'd said.

Rennae Stubbs: 'Emma, I'm fairly certain they're watching you at home. Actually, you know what, while you are here and you have that camera on you, what do you want to say to those people back home, because there's some loved ones that I'm sure are just in tears right now back in England.'

Emma: 'Yeah, thank you so much everyone. [Still laughing] Yeah, I mean, I wish you could be here with me but honestly, everything that we've been working for, it's showing here, so really thank you so much.'

Rennae Stubbs: 'Okay, so take us through the last few games. You win the set. You know that Belinda is going to fight to the end, but take us through that last game, like what are you telling yourself point by point, because you looked so composed for someone so young.'

Emma: 'Yeah, I was love thirty in my last couple of service games, so to hold was pretty big. Just played one point at a time, trying to focus on what I can control myself. Landing first serves, [pauses for crowd noise] landing first serves and Belinda's an incredibly tough opponent, so she was going to fight all the way until the end, but I'm just really pleased to have come through that.'

Rennae Stubbs: 'Okay, so there are some other players in this draw. One just turned nineteen the other day. How much inspiration are you getting from someone like Leylah [Fernandez] as well? Are you seeing each other in the locker room, saying 'hey, we're pretty good'? The inspiration that you must be getting from someone like her as well, has that helped you in this tournament?'

Emma: 'Yeah, to have so many young players here doing so well, it just shows how strong the next generation is and Leylah is doing incredibly well. She's really nice. She was passing out cupcakes for her nineteenth birthday yesterday, but yeah, everyone's on their own trajectory so I'm just here taking care of what I can control, and it's my own journey at the end of the day.'

Rennae Stubbs: 'Well, Emma, from everybody in this whole stadium and everyone around the world, congratulations. You're through to the semi-finals.'

Catherine Whitaker: 'What is happening? A qualifier, eighteen years old on her U.S. Open debut has reached the semi-final and she's British! Let's head down to Jim Courier and Tim Henman who were courtside, watching this unfold. Jim, how did Tim cope with the latter stages of that.'

Jim Courier: 'I gotta tell you, Tim was a huge assist for Emma, because at five four she served for the match. At thirty all, she doesn't look up at her team she looks straight at Tim, for like a good four seconds. So, what did you tell her, what kind of signs were you giving her?'

Tim Henman: 'I said win. When at thirty all, I said win two more points and you'll be fine.'

Catherine Whitaker: 'Jim, give us a neutral, non-British perspective on how good Emma was today.'

Jim Courier: 'What's really impressive is the fact that she goes up a level in competition today against Belinda Bencic who has as much confidence as anyone right now. Emma was able to withstand the early barrage, didn't panic, she stayed right in the mix, did her thing and at the end of the match the roles reversed. It was Bencic who really couldn't quite problem solve a way through it. Bencic got really tight at the end, she made a whole slew of unforced errors, because she knew if she didn't do something of

118

quality, Emma was going to punish her. I'm marvelling at the way that she is able to move around the court, stay down low and continue to execute the shots. Yes, it's hard to finish these matches for a young player, of course it is, but she found a way through it. It's hugely impressive and I think you can hear it here [crowd still cheering], she's captivating this American audience just like she did over in the U.K. at Wimbledon. She said in the interview with Rennae that she had to adjust and adapt, well, you know what Billie Jean King always says, "Champions adjust." She's in a great spot. There were 256 when she started in this event and it's down to the final four. There's a long way to go and whoever she plays in the next match, she's going to be the underdog, but you know, she's playing with a lot of confidence that is for sure.'

Emma is being mobbed for selfies and autographs.

Catherine Whitaker: 'Timothy, if you want to get an Emma Raducanu autograph, you're gonna have to get in the queue now because honestly there are thousands of New Yorkers just wanting to get a glimpse of her. She's dishing out all of her kit, by the looks of things, to gathering children, I mean, it's just, it's just really incredible stuff. Jim, can she win this title, is that unthinkable?'

Jim Courier: 'Listen, if she plays it point by point and uses that old cliché, her tennis right now is amazing. The fact she moves so well that she can defend on this speedy court, that's really important, then she has the offence, the tools are there. The great unknown is how does she manage the moment and that's one thing that no one ever knows until they're in the moment. If she can play the same type of tennis that's delivered eight match wins in this tournament, normally takes seven to win a major, it's going to take ten for her to do it, coz she's coming through qualies, but why not? Right? She's gotta believe in herself.'

Anne Keothavong in the studio: 'I couldn't be prouder of Emma's achievement. What another fantastic performance from her, and a straight sets victory. To win again, in the manner that she did, I don't think anyone really expected that, but she is playing such good tennis, she looks like she belongs, looks at home out there on the big stage, and if anything, just seems to get better and better with each match, which is really, yeah, incredible.'

Annabel Croft: 'Well, it's just mind-blowing, isn't it? Then again, maybe not, because of what we've seen throughout the course of this tournament. Yes, there's been a couple of nervy starts as there were in this match and the one previously, but she's a problem solver, and once she kind of figures out what's going on and she starts to relax, she started to find her flow and she totally and utterly dismantled a former world number four, today, and the current Olympic gold champion. It was interesting to see how, as rallies developed, psychologically you can see how she can get under the skin of all of the opponents that we've seen so far. They literally can't cope with the pressure that's coming at them with her tennis, she's so mentally strong, and you know Bencic's game just absolutely just evaporated. She wasn't even going for the corners, she was hitting everything down the centre of the court. She just got so tight and nervous herself out there, she really couldn't cope with it. I mean, my goodness, I think we are starting to believe she really, really could potentially go on and win these championships.'

Anne Keothavong: 'Okay, I'm going to be the voice of reason again, just keep it real. She's through to the semi-finals, and yes, we should be excited and celebrate it. It's just been a wonderful run for her.'

Such wonderful praise for Emma, quite unbelievable, which is one of the reasons I felt this book was needed, so that there was a record of how the experts opinions gradually changed over the course of the ten matches.

What's next? Later that day, Maria Sakkari, the Greek number one, won the right to play Emma in the semi-final.

9 Maria Sakkari—U.S. Open Semi-Final

Maria Sakkari is eighteenth in the world rankings, so another top twenty player. She's from Greece, five feet eight inches tall and twenty-six years old. She plays right-handed.

Emma's arrived in her now signature red and blue outfit with the same yellow sun visor from which the usual ponytail trails. Sakkari is wearing a green mottled, almost camouflage coloured skirt with a salmon top and black neck strap. Her blonde/brown hair is tied up in a topknot. Her shoes are mainly white. At the coin toss, Emma is standing calmly while Sakkari is doing huge knee jumps, trying to impose her physical prowess for which she has a reputation.

The game is under lights at the Arthur Ashe Stadium, so the balls will play slightly slower than during the day.

Marcus Buckland[xvii]: 'The temperature is seventy Fahrenheit with the humidity very high at seventy-nine percent. How do you see this, Annabel, Greg?'

Greg Rusedski: 'I'm expecting a three setter. I got the first one wrong in three sets against Fernandez, I'm hoping I get it wrong again, because I'm going for Sakkari tonight, just because she's had the more difficult [matches] and beating the bigger players in Kvitova, Andreescu, and Pliskova, and I'm feeling this is her time, but I hope I'm wrong.'

Annabel Croft: 'I'm a little bit with Greg on that one. To be honest, I thought Bencic was going to be a step up in class for her and she proved everybody wrong in that. In fact, even though she didn't get off to a great start, she started to get under Bencic's skin psychologically to the point where it completely dismantled her forehand and I'm intrigued as to whether that will happen again tonight, because I think Sakkari, as good as her forehand is, and it has rotation on it, a flatter backhand obviously, but the forehand can break down a little bit, so I'm intrigued by that but I do feel like she does have way more experience and as Greg has said, she's beaten the much, much tougher opponents to get here.'

Martina Navratilova: 'I hope they both play well. Let the better player win.'

Emma serves. On the ninth rally stroke, Emma tries to play down the line and hits the net post. Love fifteen.

Emma sees Sakkari coming to the net, tries to pass her, but hits into the net on the seventh rally stroke. Love thirty.

Deep wide ace. Fifteen thirty.

Fifth rally stroke goes long from Emma. Two breakpoints already against the teenager. Another nervy start. Fifteen forty.

Mark Petchey: 'To be the best you have to beat the best. Maria Sakkari is number thirteen in the world, but with a race ranking[xviii] of number six. That shows how great her season has been. Already a couple of breakpoints.'

Sakkari hits the fourth rally stroke long. Thirty forty. Still a breakpoint.

Emma hits a crosscourt backhand winner onto the line after Sakkari's return. Deuce. Second breakpoint saved.

Trying to hit a down the line winner, Emma hits the ninth rally stroke into the net. Third breakpoint for Sakkari.

Sakkari hits the eighth rally stroke long. Second deuce.

Strangely, Sakkari seems to have to keep pulling her skirt up and looks a little uncomfortable.

Ace down the T. Advantage Emma.

Sakkari puts the fourth rally stroke into the net. Game to Emma. One game to love.

***

They change ends, Sakkari to serve.

Incredible defence by Emma. Sakkari hit the lines twice, but Emma scampered to return each shot. Sakkari hits the ninth rally stroke into the net. Love fifteen.

Emma hits the fourth rally stroke a fraction long. Fifteen all.

Martina Navratilova in the commentary box with Mark Petchey: 'That's the right play, good, attacking the second serve. This is the right shot, just missed it long, not that much.'

Hard-hitting rally and Sakkari hits the ninth rally stroke into the net. Fifteen thirty.

Double fault. Sakkari hit a ninety-nine miles per hour second serve. She was going for too much. Fifteen forty. Emma has two breakpoints.

Emma gets to the third rally stroke from Sakkari who had come in and attempted a dropshot. It falls short into the net. Emma pumps her fist at her team box. She's broken Sakkari. Two-love.

Martina Navratilova: 'She did not get one first serve in. Nice start for Emma. Great start, in fact.'

***

Third game. Emma begins her serve routine.

Forehand crosscourt winner from Sakkari on the fourth rally stroke. Love fifteen.

Mark Petchey: 'One of the heaviest hitters on the tour. That's a mean ball she strikes when you're up the other end. Very Spanish set up with the racquet, with all the weight in the head and she's strong enough to wield it, as well. Not everybody is.'

Another great crosscourt winner from Sakkari on the sixth rally stroke. Love thirty. Is she going to break straight back?

Emma hits Sakkari's return a fraction long. She was surprised to hear the call. Three breakpoints. Love forty.

Emma watches the Hawkeye replay and it actually shows as longer than it looked. Must admit, it looked in to me.

Good second serve from Emma saves one breakpoint as Sakkari's return finds the net. Fifteen forty.

Emma serves extremely wide, forcing a high return. Emma's backhand volley is too strong and Sakkari hits into the net. Two breakpoints saved. Thirty forty.

Sakkari misses the line badly with the sixth rally stroke. Deuce.

Martina Navratilova: 'Sakkari is oh for six in break points, the first two games. That can get into your head, specially I mean both counts, fifteen forty and then love forty but it can create some scar tissue mentally.'

Emma hits the fifth rally stroke long. A fourth breakpoint.

Massive serve down the T. Sakkari hits the net. She's still hoisting up her skirt between points. Second deuce.

Great wide second serve and the return hits the net. Advantage Emma.

Martina Navratilova: 'Terrific second serve out wide, ninety miles per hour. That's as good as some women's first serve.'

Emma hits the line on the fifth rally stroke, but Sakkari manages to return it. Emma's next shot lands behind Sakkari who guessed wrong. Can this be real? Three games to love.

Mark Petchey: 'Sakkari guesses, expecting a ball into her forehand. It wasn't the greatest of shots, but it didn't need to be. It is the greatest of starts for Raducanu, three straight games at the start of this semi-final.'

**

Sakkari speaks to the umpire, then grabs a new skirt from her bag, reads the label on it and runs off the court pursued by a court official. Meanwhile, Emma sits quietly, opening a bottle of pink liquid and holding the portable air conditioning hose under her other arm, playing the cool air over her neck and face.

Sakkari is back and *still* hoisting up her skirt's waistband. Looks like she needs to shorten the waistband with a safety pin.

Sakkari to serve.

For once, she gets a first serve in and Emma's return is not good enough. Sakkari plays a crosscourt forehand winner. Fifteen love.

Martina Navratilova: 'I think she was complaining about her skirt was too big, but this one seems to be too. I don't know.'

Emma's return is played into the net by Sakkari. Fifteen all.

Sakkari double faults. Fifteen thirty.

Another first serve in, and Emma's return flies long. Thirty all.

First serve again. Emma struggles to return. The ball goes high over the net and Sakkari rushing in, forehand smashes the third rally stroke close to the line. Forty thirty.

Sakkari's mother is applauding and Martina Navratilova comments: 'She must be so nervous. I know what my mum used to go through. She would close her eyes. She would wear sunglasses, so people didn't know that she had her eyes closed. So nervous, don't admit the parents at all.'

The rally begins with ground strokes, but Emma suddenly increases the weight on two shots, the second of which causes Sakkari to play a weak shot. Emma runs into the net and plays a great forehand just over the net and the Greek can't reach it. Deuce.

Martina Navratilova: 'Beautiful! A solid volley. I was actually looking at Emma's technique in the warm-up on the volley, and it's really immaculate. She just doesn't have a weakness in her game, and when you're technically that sound, when you get nervous, the technique holds you together, but that was a really nice touch as well, taking the pace off. Not a drop volley but a kind of a neut volley. Perfect. I call it the neut. It's not a fully formed volley.'

Emma's sixth stroke of the rally finds the line and has Sakkari at full stretch forcing her shot to fly well long. Emma has breakpoint. She screams, 'Yes!' down the length of the court.

A fantastic return from Emma, but Sakkari digs it out from beneath her feet and it puts Emma off balance and her shot hits the net. Deuce number two.

A short return from Emma is sent back onto the line. Advantage Sakkari.

Emma skies her return. Sakkari waits for it to fall and her forehand flies way beyond the court. Third deuce.

Mark Petchey: 'Well, that is the sort of shot which erodes your confidence in a big match.'

Emma's backhand down the line catches the line on the fourth rally stroke, leaving Sakkari stranded. She's also unhappy with the lack of an out call. A replay shows the ball has clearly hit the line. With automatic Hawkeye in operation, there are no bad calls. Breakpoint again.

Double fault. It's astonishing. Four games to love for Emma.

***

Mark Petchey: 'Raducanu is winning all the big points, all the right points, she's doing all the right things, and the dream continues for Raducanu, but this, in the opening set, at least for Sakkari, is turning into somewhat of a nightmare here.'

Emma to serve.

Good return from Sakkari and Emma's backhand goes wide trying to hit the winner. Love fifteen.

The third stroke of the rally sees Emma land the crosscourt on the line. Emma has her out of position and Sakkari hits the sixth rally stroke into the net. Fifteen all.

Martina Navratilova: 'Fifteen unforced errors for Sakkari so far. That was one of them.'

Good serve down the T causes Sakkari's return to fly well long. Thirty fifteen.

Another overhit forehand return. Forty fifteen.

There's a liquid spill at the seats and it is being cleared up before play can continue. Seems to have been Sakkari's portable air-conditioning device.

Emma plays a dropshot on the third rally stroke, but it wasn't good enough and Sakkari hit it straight back at Emma. She just managed to get her racquet onto it and Sakkari fired a rushed shot long. Everything seems to be going Emma's way. Emma's still in dreamland. Five games to love.

***

Mark Petchey: 'Even after a woeful attempted dropshot, it is only her side of the scoreboard that is ticking over so far in this opening set. Five love. Scarcely believable.'

Martina Navratilova: 'It looked like this was going to be the score-line at fifteen forty in the first game, but as she did against Shelby Rogers as well, down love two, love forty, wins eleven games in a row and she's been down in her service games two out of three matches, but she's held her nerve and Sakkari is scratching her head, right now. She's not sure what's happening.'

Five straight games for the teenager. Sakkari will need to serve to stop the bagel.

A heavy return sets up for Emma to hit a backhand winner down the line, on the line, on rally stroke four. Love fifteen.

Martina Navratilova: 'The matches before, Sakkari was getting like forty percent of her serves unreturned. Raducanu is getting ninety-three percent of the balls in play when Sakkari is serving. She's just not used to that, so she has to work a lot harder on her second shot and afterwards, of course. The nerves are definitely playing a part here.'

One hundred and eleven miles per hour ace down the T. Fifteen all.

Dramatic rally. Sakkari only just getting to a lob on the line from Emma, but then hitting a sixth rally shot crosscourt forehand winner. The Greek is gesticulating to her box as the replay shows the ball hit the line by only a millimetre or two. Thirty fifteen.

Emma hits the fourth stroke of the rally into the net and a huge shout is emitted by Sakkari. Forty fifteen.

Martina Navratilova: 'Trying to get herself fired up, trying to get the crowd fired up. She hasn't had any opportunity, really, to get them going.'

Double fault. Forty thirty.

The fourth rally stroke is overhit wide by Emma, but only by millimetres. Sakkari has saved the bagel. She's still shouting and gesticulating towards her team's box. Five-one.

**

Emma to serve.

An eighteen-stroke baseline rally. Sakkari hits wide. Fifteen love.

Mark Petchey: 'Just incredible movement, balance, length [of shot], and that is a heavy ball, as I keep stressing, coming at her as well.'

Martina Navratilova: 'She's made the adjustment beautifully. She gets in position really well, so she is balanced when she's hitting the ball, she's not stretching, she's not reaching, she's not going backwards. Sakkari did a good job there with that change-up, then got the ball she wanted, but missed it.'

Emma hits Sakkari's deep return long A rare, unforced error. Fifteen all.

Beautiful, deep serve out wide to the Greek's forehand. Sakkari's return flies high and long. Thirty fifteen.

Emma's second serve hits the line and Sakkari's return finds the net. Two set points. Forty fifteen.

Another deep serve out wide and Sakkari fires long. First set to Emma in the semi-final of the U.S. Open, by an incredible six games to one.

***

Mark Petchey: 'The dream is very much alive for Raducanu, dropping just the one game, and in our wildest dreams, Tim, we couldn't have expected that.'

Tim Henman, courtside: 'No, definitely not. Her poise and persistence, the way that she's dictated play, how cleanly she struck the ball from the word go, an unbelievable set of tennis. It's been Raducanu who has just dominated the big points. I'm expecting a big reaction from Sakkari. She's looked unsettled, there's been quite a lot of dialogue between herself and her box at the end of that first set. This is where she's going to have to show some experience and try to dig her heels in, and wrestle the momentum from Raducanu, as she has been absolutely faultless so far. So, the ideal start, can she maintain the momentum in this second set?'

Sakkari to serve.

A wide first serve—Emma's return flies long. Fifteen love.

Sakkari's fifth shot of the rally tips the net and drops over to oohs and aahs from the crowd. Thirty love.

Solid serve that Emma hits into the net. Forty love.

An ace down the T. Sakkari's immediately on the scoreboard in the second set. Has the recovery begun? Love-one.

***

They change ends. Emma to serve.

Fifth shot of the rally. Emma steps into the court and fires a backhand down the line. Fifteen love.

Emma overhits the ninth shot of the rally. It goes long. Fifteen all.

Very wide serve begins a seven-shot rally, which finishes with a terrific forehand volley from Emma onto Sakkari's backhand line, leaving the Greek player stranded on the baseline. Thirty fifteen.

Martina Navratilova: 'Wow! What a volley.'

Oh, Emma double faults. Thirty all.

Sakkari fires the eighth rally stroke long and hits the returning ball hard in annoyance. Emma shouts out to her team, 'Yes!' Forty thirty.

On the ninth rally stroke, Emma hits a slice onto Sakkari's forehand line, and the reply is mistimed wide. One game all.

Martina Navratilova: 'Nice change up from Emma. First slice she's hit, and it paid dividends. Floater into the corner and Sakkari mistimed it. That's why changing of the pace, or the spin is so effective. Takes the opponent out of rhythm.'

***

Sakkari serving. Good return from Emma and Sakkari hits the net. Love fifteen.

Martina Navratilova: 'Raducanu keeps attacking that second serve, not going for too much, hitting it hard down the middle, hopefully deep. She's drawn a lot of errors that way.'

Emma's return is too ambitious and goes wide. Fifteen all.

Emma attacks the second serve and hits a backhand crosscourt winner. More fist-pumping towards her team box. Fifteen thirty.

Sakkari hits the fifth stroke long. Two breakpoints for Emma.

Mark Petchey: 'The problem is for Sakkari right now, she can't exactly see her way through. Her forehand down the line goes into Emma's most secure shot, she's over pressing, trying to get some results going that way.'

Martina Navratilova: 'And even when she does play a good shot, good rally, Emma's there coz she moves so well. She's really been able to neutralise the Sakkari power. I think that's why the errors are coming in.'

A massive return from Emma, which Sakkari fires very long indeed. Emma has the break. 'Wow! Look at that,' says Martina Navratilova.'

Two-one.

***

Mark Petchey, as Emma comes out to serve: 'She's captured the imagination of not just the British fans, but American and global fans as well, and she is on the cusp of something truly extraordinary.'

An unreturnable wide serve. Fifteen love.

Emma double faults and skips into the air with annoyance at herself. Fifteen all.

On the ninth rally stroke, Emma hits a great backhand down the line. Sakkari reaches it, but Emma easily fires the winner behind her as Sakkari runs the wrong way across the baseline. Thirty fifteen.

Martina Navratilova: 'What a shot that backhand down the line is. Beautiful play and then again, so quick off the mark, she smells that it's going to be a short ball coming back. She's moving forward and Sakkari's too-short crosscourt and Emma's right on top of this one, beautiful.'

Sakkari tries to come into the net and Emma's backhand crosscourt passes her. Forty fifteen.

Martina Navratilova: 'Again, Raducanu neutralising good shots from Sakkari.'

Ace down the T. She's consolidated the break. Three games to one.

***

Sakkari serving.

Mark Petchey: 'Well, it is just simply amazing to watch, isn't it? Breathtaking!'

Emma hits the sixth rally stroke wide. Fifteen love.

Emma's return is hard and deep, forcing Sakkari to hit long. Fifteen all.

Martina Navratilova: 'This is danger time for Maria Sakkari. She really can't afford to lose her serve again.'

A despondent Sakkari, has a let serve, then fault, then serves into the net. Double fault. Fifteen thirty.

On the eleventh rally stroke, Sakkari attempts a dropshot and it falls into the net. Emma has two more breakpoints. Fifteen forty.

Emma's forehand return of an excellent wide serve flies long. Thirty forty.

Emma mishits the twelfth rally stroke. Deuce.

One hundred and twelve miles per hour ace down the T. Advantage Sakkari.

Fourth shot of the rally sees Emma hit into the net while trying to play down the line. Over ambitious. Sakkari is shaking her fist and shouting at herself. She knew she had to win that game. Three-two.

Mark Petchey: 'Big hold of serve. You can see how much belief that has given Sakkari as well. She stays in contention.'

***

Emma serving.

Good serve, even better return, but Emma hits a backhand down the line behind Sakkari. Fifteen love.

Good solid twelve stroke rally ends with Sakkari firing wide. Thirty love.

Good serve, not a bad return, but Emma rushes it and hits a backhand crosscourt winner. Forty love.

131

Another first serve, a powerful return into Emma's backhand, but she just wallops it down the line. It is just clipped by Sakkari's racquet. Love game to Emma. Four-two.

Martina Navratilova: 'That is a massive hold for Raducanu, not blinking at all. Holds at love, just snuffing any kind of momentum that Sakkari was building.'

***

Lots of crowd noise and Emma's coach and team are pumping their fists. The umpire must call for quiet, as Sakkari prepares to serve.

Martina Navratilova: 'This is a must-hold for Sakkari, the way Emma has been serving.'

Emma is matching Sakkari, stroke for stroke until the Greek player hits the ninth rally shot into the net. Love fifteen.

More calls for quiet from the umpire.

Emma has Sakkari on the run and the Greek hits the fifth rally shot into the net. Love thirty.

Emma's return is too good and Sakkari hits long. Three breakpoints for the teenager. Love forty.

Sakkari is shouting at her team's box. Her mother looks grim faced in the stand. Emma, waiting at the other end is lecturing herself on what to do and what not to do with these triple breakpoints.

Good defensive play by Sakkari and Emma hits the eighth stroke of the rally into the net. Two breakpoints remaining. Fifteen forty.

Martina Navratilova: 'Still on the edge of the ledge here. Fifteen forty. Not looking good for her, but she keeps fighting.'

Superb deep, wide ace. Thirty forty.

What a rally, the crowd is oohing and aahing throughout it. The ninth shot is a dropshot by Sakkari, Emma's speed gets her to it, but she's right at the net and Sakkari lobs her with stroke eleven. Emma charges back and manages to sky the ball back to the other court. Sakkari hits a forehand smash into Emma's forehand corner. She just reaches it and skies it again. Sakkari smashes it into Emma's backhand corner. The teenager scampers across and skies it again. This time, Sakkari makes no mistake, and on the seventeenth stroke, smashes it into Emma's forehand side leaving the Brit stranded mid court. Deuce.

Mark Petchey: 'Oh, have you ever seen anything like it. One of the most extraordinary points, in one of the biggest moments in a match.'

Martina Navratilova: 'Both players giving it absolutely everything. Raducanu defending so well, making Sakkari hit so many more balls. Finally, Sakkari puts it away, but what a rally that was. So physical!'

Emma's devasting forehand crosscourt return forces Sakkari to hit long. Another breakpoint.

Martina Navratilova: 'The nerve of this young woman is just amazing. She has such belief in her game.'

Emma saves a brilliant shot into the corner, but Sakkari courageously hits back to the same place while Emma's running the other way. Second deuce.

The eighth rally shot sees Emma miss the line by millimetres. Advantage Sakkari.

Martina Navratilova: 'Just missed it, could've been a winner. Sakkari is defending really well now. Emma maybe pressing a little bit, but Sakkari is defending better.'

Blistering backhand crosscourt return forces Sakkari to hit long. The Greek player is shaking her head in despair. Third deuce.

Mark Petchey: 'Well, we always thought Victoria Azarenka was arguably one of the best returners in the last decade or so of the tennis ball, but I've gotta say that Emma Raducanu, tonight, has been pinging the ball to Sakkari's baseline with unnerving accuracy and repetition.'

Sakkari hits the fifth rally stroke into the net. Advantage and breakpoint number five to Emma.

Massive second serve from Sakkari, ninety-nine miles per hour into the corner, and she goes on to play a crosscourt winner on the fifth rally stroke. Fourth deuce.

Another good serve, and Emma returns wide. Advantage Sakkari.

Sakkari serves and Emma's return goes into the net. A ten-minute game is over. Sakkari lets out a frightening roar. Four-three.

***

Emma comes out after the break to serve. Still a set and break up.

Sakkari's return goes long. Fifteen love.

This time, the return goes into the net. Thirty love.

Martina Navratilova: 'She just keeps getting those first serves in. She's changing locations so well. Sakkari can't read the serve and she can't guess, and when she doesn't guess then she doesn't react fast enough.'

Deep serve into Sakkari's forehand, Emma puts a backhand into the same location behind the Greek player, she's off-balance and hits into the net. Forty love.

Umpire calls for quiet again.

Some idiot shouts, 'Emma!' just as she tosses the ball and has to compose herself again. Who does that fan think he's helping?

Martina Navratilova: 'Come on, people. There's one in every crowd!'

An eighth rally stroke forehand crosscourt winner from Sakkari lands on the line. Forty fifteen.

Good return from Sakkari and Emma hits too hard into the net. Forty thirty.

Emma waits patiently for the crowd to quieten, looking around the stadium.

A very solid rally, but Sakkari overhits the tenth shot. Game to Emma. Now five games to three.

***

Martina Navratilova: 'Emma needed that unforced error, she was playing a little too carefully there, but got the hold anyway.'

Sakkari to serve. Emma hits the sixth stroke into the net. Fifteen love.

Sakkari slams a short return behind the Brit. Thirty love.

Fourth rally stroke slice from Emma forces Sakkari to overhit wide. Thirty fifteen.

Sakkari has a net fluke, which Emma manages to reach but hits long. Forty fifteen.

Emma hits a great forehand return off a deep, wide serve. Sakkari hits the next shot wide. Forty thirty.

Emma has trouble returning another deep, wide serve and Sakkari smashes the winner. She's not going to give the match to the Brit without a fight. Five-four.

***

Emma is going to have to serve for the match and Sakkari knows that it is her last chance to recover the break. The crowd buzzes with anticipation while the players are in their seats.

Mark Petchey: 'Great tenacity shown by Sakkari throughout the course of this second set to keep herself in contention, to keep her own personal dream alive. One service game, Martina.'

Martina Navratilova: 'Sakkari hasn't broken yet, though much closer in the first set. Couldn't do it big time. Raducanu serving for the final of the U.S. Open. Needless to say, never been here before, so will she be able to hold her nerve? Fortune favours the brave and it also favours the young coz they tend to be more brave, because they don't know everything that can go wrong! Got their whole life in front of them—fearless. Emma needs to be fearless here.'

Mark Petchey: 'Exponentially, the pressure, the opportunity, the goal, the dream, everything converging into this moment. It doesn't get much bigger than this.'

Emma serving for a place in the final of the U.S. Open Grand Slam. The crowd noise continues. Emma looks around the enormous stadium, gazing at the wall of faces, no doubt spotting some union flags being waved by the faithful Brits.

'Thank you, the players are ready,' says the umpire.

Emma hits the ninth stroke wide. Love fifteen.

Sakkari returns into the net. Emma bends double and screams, 'Come on!' Fifteen all.

Emma hits a forehand winner down the line. Thirty fifteen.

Martina Navratilova: 'That's a gutsy shot there. It looked a bit of a push, but good enough push. Tough shots to time when you're nervous. She did it.'

A hard-hitting rally with Emma hitting a great forehand down the line on the eleventh rally stroke. Sakkari replies into the net. Two match points. Emma blows on her hand as she runs for the towel. Forty fifteen.

Mark Petchey: 'If you stayed up late into the early morning in the U.K., this is the moment you've been waiting for, Raducanu serving for a place in U.S. Open final.'

A super wide serve into Sakkari's forehand, returned by the Greek and Emma hits down the open court. Sakkari returns it very high, and Emma smashes a forehand winner behind her opponent.

Game set and match to Emma Raducanu. Six one, six four. She's through to the U.S. Open final. Unbelievable! She throws her racquet down as she finishes the smash and raises her hands to the top of her head as if it needs to be held on. Perhaps, it does. She thanks Sakkari for the game then, smiling and then laughing outright in joy as she turns towards her team box.

Mark Petchey: 'Emma Raducanu, you are through to the final of U.S. Open. Congratulations.'

Martina Navratilova: 'It's a woman's tournament and we have two teenagers in it. How fantastic. Raducanu's just solid. She's been here before, in another life, I mean, there's no way you can do this first time out. Such poise, on and off the court.'

Mark Petchey: 'This is her moment. This is her night. She is something else.'

Rennae Stubbs calls Emma over for the on-court interview: 'Well, I just keep saying this. All week long, ladies and gentlemen, you have just witnessed history tonight. This young woman, Emma, has just become the first qualifier in history, men's or women's, to reach a final of a major. [Huge crowd noise] Emma it must feel like an eternity

136

ago that you played in the first round of qualifying here. Can you explain the feelings you are going through right now, after qualifying and today?'

Emma: 'Honestly, that I'm here in New York has gone so fast. I've just been taking care of each day and before you know it, three weeks later, I'm in the final, and I can't actually believe it. Thanks to everyone.'

Huge applause and cheers ring out.

Rennae Stubbs: 'Emma, you've got a couple of great British players here. You've got, of course, over there, Mister Tim Henman, and Virginia Wade who is in the president's box, who was the last British woman to win the U.S. Open, but you looked at Tim on match point, just before you served. Why did you look at him?'

Emma: 'Well, Tim is honestly, such a big inspiration, like he's been helping me, telling me to treat one point at a time, and in moments like this you definitely can't get ahead of yourself, and you really need to just stay in the present, so, yeah, I'm really grateful for him and everything that he's done for British tennis and for me.'

More cheering.

Rennae Stubbs: 'Your crew up there, I saw them before the match and I just said to them, do you think it helped that the match previous was a big upset as well, and we did not expect Leylah to be in the final, but she played such a great match. Did it give you inspiration walking out here knowing that you could also do this?'

Emma: 'Honestly, today, I wasn't thinking about anyone else except for myself,' she laughs out loud, 'but while I have the moment, I really just wanna thank my team, and the LTA[xix] and everyone back home for all their help and all of their support over the years. I wouldn't be here without it.'

More incredible applause.

Rennae Stubbs: 'Walking out onto the court, Emma, this crowd has been so incredible, and you have used the crowd so well over the last couple of weeks. What inspiration is it for you to walk onto the biggest stage in tennis and use that. And how do you block it out as well.'

Emma: 'Honestly, since I've been here in New York, from my first round qualies match, I've had unbelievable support in New York and you guys have made me feel right at home today.'

More cheers of adoration. She continues, when the noise dies down, 'To play today, playing under the lights on Arthur Ashe Stadium in New York, is, honestly, one of the most iconic things in tennis, so I was just so excited to come out here and play in front of you guys, and thank you for coming.'

Yet more cheers and applause.

Rennae Stubbs: 'Final question, Emma, you are going against someone who is your age in the final of the U.S. Open, how do you manage now all the expectation and the excitement over the next twenty-four hours.'

Emma smiles and chuckles devilishly: 'I mean, is there any expectation? I'm a qualifier, so technically, on paper, there is nothing, no pressure on me.' She breaks down in laughter.

Rennae Stubbs: 'Well, I hate to tell you this, Emma, but it's going to be a massive crowd here to enjoy an incredible, incredible women's final in a couple of days. Ladies and gentlemen, the first qualifier ever through to a major final— Emma Raducanu!'

A joyful cacophony ensues.

Marcus Buckland in the studio: 'Annabel and Greg, I don't make some exaggeration to say you sat there open-mouthed at the way in which she set about dismantling Maria Sakkari.'

Greg Rusedski: 'I was dumbfounded. I mean, this was something special we just saw here from Emma Raducanu. That performance is worthy of a world number one, a multiple Grand Slam champion, the calmness, the composure, the belief, the handling of the big points. This is her first ever semi-final of a major and it was like she's playing the first round of this event. It was astonishing!'

138

Marcus Buckland: 'These are moments she will never forget, but you sense she may have plenty more of them, the way she started here.'

Annabel Croft: 'It certainly feels like that, doesn't it? I never expected the match to turn out the way that it did. I thought that Sakkari would come out and really compete and give her a run for her money, but she was like all the rest of them that have been slayed along the way. She, literally, could not cope with the ball striking, the timing, the precision, the beautiful serving and the absolutely outmanoeuvring of her at all costs. It was great to see Andrew Richardson, her coach in their corner up there just supporting, and all the emotion that they've been through, my goodness they must have been through quite a lot.'

Marcus Buckland: 'You could see in Emma's eyes that she was drinking it all in and Andrew Richardson has stayed very calm throughout the fortnight, but he let it go there for a moment.'

Greg Rusedski: 'I don't blame him one bit whatsoever. He has done a fantastic job with Emma, as well as all the coaches she's worked with, and what I loved about the speeches as well, she thanked her team, she thanked the LTA for their support throughout the years. She's really got everything. You know, when you talk about superstars, she has what you call *it*.'

10 Leylah Fernandez—U.S. Open Final

Leylah Annie Fernandez, nineteen at the time of the final, was born in Montreal and is just a couple of months older than Emma. Her father, Jorge, was a former footballer and hails from Ecuador. Her mother, Irene, is a Filipino Canadian. Leylah has been a professional tennis player since July 2019. In 2021 she won the Monterrey Open and, at the time of the match with Raducanu, she was ranked number seventy-three in the world.

To reach the final, Fernandez had the far more difficult route, beating world number three, Naomi Osaka, world number seventeen, Angelique Kerber, world number five, Elina Svitolina, and the biggest of her achievements, beating world number two Aryna Sabalenka, one of the biggest hitters in the game, in the semi-final.

Emma, once again, is wearing her NY Slam outfit in red and blue with her yellow visor and will be using her Wilson Steam 100 racquet painted as a Blade. Fernandez is wearing an indigo tank top with a magenta stripe, and a flouncy white tennis skirt. She has opted not to wear a hat or visor. She plays left-handed with a Babolat Pure Aero racquet.

Before walking onto the Arthur Ashe court, Emma answered questions at a pre-final interview in the players' tunnel. She is asked what gave her the belief that she could be there, today, at a U.S. Open final.

Emma: 'I think I just believe in myself in general, and the time is flying here in New York. Just been taking it one match at a time and it's got me to the final, so gonna go out there and enjoy it today.'

She was then asked how she would describe the opportunity.

Emma: 'Yeah, I mean, it's so exciting to be in my second Grand Slam and in the final. I can't really believe it, but yeah, I'm going out there today and I can't wait to just get stuck in. I'm sure the crowd will be great, so it will be a really positive experience.'

Anne Keothavong[xx] in the studio: 'It has just been surreal, I mean, I cannot believe we're sat here talking about Emma Raducanu, it's just been an outstanding performance, match after match, has been able to raise her level, she's been able to embrace the occasion, and she's been able to win fans over as well with her tennis, with her smile and her charm. She's got so much going for her and this is a huge moment for sport also.'

Greg Rudeski in the studio: 'Let's look at the history. No qualifier in the men's or women's game has been in a Grand Slam final before. I mean, it is quite tremendous. I agree with everything you said there, Anne, but let's not also forget her opponent. Her opponent had no form whatsoever coming into this event. She hadn't won back-to-back matches all the way since March, so we've got the next generation, an eighteen year old against a nineteen year old. This is rather exciting.'

Anne Keothavong: 'This is unbelievable. This is only Emma's fourth WTA, or big tournament. She was ranked outside the world's top three hundred just a few months ago, and this run no one could have predicted. You know. I knew she was good, lots of people knew she was good, and she was an exceptional talent, but no one expected this type of rise from Emma.'

Greg Rusedski: 'This is unprecedented. I mean, you look at the history books. Only one other player in their second ever major tournament has been to the finals and that was Pam Shriver. No player in their first two events has ever gone on to win a slam in the women's game and also you put her in categories of names of players to get there as well, to get to at least the fourth round in their two majors, you're talking Chrissie Evert, world number one, Monica Seles, world number one, and you're talking Jennifer Capriati, world number one, so she's in immense company right now, creating history.'

On the court for the ball toss, Emma is standing alongside Billie Jean King and other women tennis players who saw the rise of the women's game in the modern era, leading to equality with the men's game.

It's ideal conditions. Cloudy, 75F, 37% humidity. The stadium is full, over twenty thousand spectators. The warm-up is over.

Emma gathers the balls and prepares to serve.

First blood to Fernandez with a sixth rally stroke backhand crosscourt winner. Love fifteen.

Fernandez hits into the net on the sixth rally stroke, trying to go crosscourt again. Fifteen all.

Emma keeps trying to play to the leftie, Fernandez's forehand and eventually the returned ball comes high. Emma runs in and plays a forehand winner into the same part of the court, but unreachable. Great play. Thirty fifteen.

Fernandez returns into the net. Forty fifteen.

Emma hits Fernandez's return into the net. Forty thirty.

Good serve into Fernandez's forehand, then Emma plays a backhand, crosscourt winner. The scoreboard is ticking. One-love.

***

Fernandez serving.

A second serve is punished by Emma's backhand winner into the advantage side. Love fifteen.

Double fault. Love thirty.

Great return from Emma, and Fernandez hits the crosscourt shot wide. Three breakpoints for the Brit. Love Forty.

Emma hits the sixth stroke of a very central rally, long. Fifteen forty.

Emma was having the best of the rally, but Fernandez managed to hit a forehand behind her on the eleventh rally stroke. Thirty forty.

Mark Petchey: 'What an impressive point. Fernandez so impressive in defence.'

Emma's crosscourt return flies wide. Three breakpoints saved by the Canadian. Deuce.

Exciting rally. Emma pins Fernandez to her backhand corner until a loopy ball comes over the net. She rushes into the net, but doesn't quite play a winner and a second high ball is returned. Emma prepares and hits an unreachable backhand volley into the same corner on the eighth rally stroke. Fourth breakpoint.

Ace down the T. Deuce.

Double fault. Breakpoint number five.

Emma hits the eighth stroke of the rally into the net. Third deuce.

Emma's return into the net. Advantage Fernandez.

Fernandez hits a down the line shot, which Emma scrambles to return, but the Canadian then fires the reply, the seventh rally stroke, wide. Fourth deuce.

Martina Navratilova: 'She does the hard work, then misses the easy one.'

Fernandez plays a great shot into Emma's forehand corner then rushes the return forcing the error on the twelfth stroke of the rally. To be fair, both the ninth and eleventh shots from the Canadian deserved to win the point, but Emma is so fast. Advantage to Fernandez.

Hard-hitting from Emma and Fernandez hits the seventh rally stroke long. Deuce number five.

Great rally with each player having the other running back and forth along the baseline. Fernandez makes the error on the thirteenth rally stroke and the ball goes wide. A sixth breakpoint for Emma. The game is approaching ten minutes.

Wonderful return and Fernandez's forehand finds the net. Emma has the first break. Two-love.

***

Emma serving. Emma hits the seventh rally stroke into the net after a fine rally from both women. Love fifteen.

Good forehand from Emma into the forehand side of Fernandez's court causes an overhit shot to go long. Fifteen all.

Two backhands down the line have Fernandez scrambling and the eighth rally stroke flies long from the Canadian again. Thirty fifteen.

Martina Navratilova: 'I thought she was favourite because of just the numbers, as well as how she plays, and she's shown, so far that the match is on her racquet. She is the one dictating, she's the one pushing the envelope. If she doesn't beat herself, she should win this match. We'll see if Leylah Fernandez can get little more aggressive, but not easy to do against the really fluid power of Raducanu.'

A good crosscourt shot brings the error from Emma, hitting wide on the seventh rally stroke. Thirty all.

Emma hits the fifth rally stroke long. Breakpoint for Fernandez. Thirty forty.

Mark Petchey: 'Raducanu is currently on a streak of nineteen held service games. In danger of losing that streak here as Fernandez looks to bounce back from dropping her opening service game.'

Great serve down the T and Fernandez can only reply into the net. Deuce.

Emma hits Fernandez's return into the net. Another breakpoint for the Canadian.

A twelve-stroke rally, with Fernandez eventually hitting the net. Second deuce.

Great return from Fernandez leads to Emma being beaten on the fourth rally stroke. Breakpoint number three.

Good deep, wide ninety-seven miles per hour second serve into Fernandez's forehand side and she fires the return into the net. Another breakpoint saved. Deuce.

Double fault. Fourth breakpoint.

Emma puts the seventh rally stroke into the net and Fernandez has broken back. Two-one.

***

Fernandez serving.

Emma's return hits the net. Fifteen love.

Emma hits the fourth rally stroke into the net. Thirty love.

Fernandez plays a dropshot on the seventh rally stroke. Emma can't reach it. Forty love.

Emma's backhand down the line has Fernandez scrambling and the Brit runs in to smash a forehand volley into the open court. Forty fifteen.

On the eighth rally stroke, Emma hits a loopy shot, which was clearly going wide, but Fernandez ran into the tramlines to smash a crosscourt forehand winner, but it went long. Forty thirty.

Great serve, which Emma cannot return. Two games all.

***

Emma serving. Fernandez hits the eighth rally stroke down the line. She seems to be getting the upper hand in the rallies. Love Fifteen.

Double fault. Love thirty.

Great one-two from Emma. Fifteen thirty.

Fernandez's return flies long. Thirty all.

Fernandez's return is wide and long. Emma screams, 'Come on!' Forty thirty.

Serve down the T leaves Fernandez hitting long owing to the change of pace. Three-two.

***

Mark Petchey: 'How significant will that hold prove to be. Down love thirty. A wonderful sequence of four points for Raducanu, starting with a gorgeous forehand.'

Martina Navratilova: 'Certainly the nerves have not been shown by either player now. Maybe it'll show up at the end of the match when somebody gets closer to winning, but so far, they are both just stellar with their mentality. It's like they turned up to just play the match, oh, by the way there's about twenty thousand people watching, and the whole country of Canada and the whole country of the U.K. is watching, but no problem, I'm just going to play juniors, so it's just not the junior match. Beautiful stuff.'

Fernandez to serve.

Great return from Emma and Fernandez hits into the net. Love fifteen.

Emma hits the fourth rally stroke long. Annoyed with herself. Fifteen all.

She's still talking to herself about it as she awaits the next serve.

Double fault. Fifteen thirty.

The sixth rally stroke was an attempt at a down the line winner, which only missed marginally from Emma. Thirty all.

Emma's return into the net. Forty thirty.

Brilliant return, but Fernandez's shot hits the net cord and rolls over. The Canadian teenager signals sorry to Emma then fist-pumps to her box! Sorry, but not sorry. Three games all.

***

Emma to serve.

Great crosscourt winner for Fernandez on the eighth rally stroke. Love fifteen.

A sixteenth rally stroke dropshot from Fernandez, but Emma gets there. The next ball back from the Canadian is at the perfect height for Emma to hit the forehand volley winner. Her box stands and applauds, as does Billie Jean King who is zeroed in upon by the television camera. She's watching the match intently. Fifteen all.

Mark Petchey: 'Some lovely nuances from Raducanu early on, her box standing in ovation. You can see how Raducanu gave up a little ground there behind the baseline to get a bit more height on the ball. You can't do that while you're hugging your own baseline. She regained the territory. Clinical finish.'

Emma messed up the point, should have killed it off on the sixth rally stroke, but it came back high, and she smashed well long. Fifteen thirty.

Good second serve, which Fernandez hits into the net. Thirty all.

Good serve returned well, and Emma hit a backhand crosscourt shot. Fernandez got it back at full stretch and Emma could hit a forehand down the line winner. She screams out some words drowned out by the crowd noise. Forty thirty.

An amazing sixteen stroke rally. Game to Emma. A really important hold. Four-three.

***

Martina Navratilova: 'Wow! What precision work, depth with guts.'

Mark Petchey: 'She's a revelation.'

The umpire calls for new balls. The first time in over forty minutes of play. What a match.

Martina Navratilova: 'We're watching two future hall of famers. The only way they don't get there is if they get injured and they can't play so much. Pleasure to watch.'

Fernandez double faults. Love fifteen.

Ace down the T. Fifteen all.

Incredible forehand crosscourt return from Emma off a deep serve. Fernandez can only play into the net. Fifteen thirty.

Emma can't cleanly hit Fernandez's fifth rally shot and the ball skids off wide. Thirty all.

Emma skies the return and Fernandez hits a forehand winner into the opposite side of the court. Forty thirty.

Fernandez hits the fifth rally stroke wide, trying to go for too much. Deuce.

Good one-two from Fernandez. Her advantage.

Huge wide serve and Emma's return goes long. Game to Fernandez. Four games all.

***

Emma to serve.

One-two for Emma, finishing with a backhand crosscourt winner. Fifteen love.

A sixth rally stroke dropshot from Fernandez is too good. Fifteen all.

Fernandez gets to Emma's shot but hits the fourth rally stroke long. Thirty fifteen.

Fernandez's third rally stroke is high. Emma runs in and waits for it to bounce before hitting a backhand crosscourt shot, which the Canadian hits into the forehand side of her opponent. Emma volleys it back crosscourt and Fernandez

147

plays a down the line pass, which Emma leaves. It flies just long. She pumps her fist at her team. Forty fifteen.

Fernandez's fourth rally stroke is long. Game to Emma. Five-four.

***

Mark Petchey: 'Everything we could have wished this to have been.'

Fernandez serves and sends back a deep shot off Emma's return and the Brit's lob doesn't reach the net. Fifteen love.

Good deep return straight down the middle and Fernandez hits it long. Fifteen all.

Martina Navratilova: 'Close. Absolutely nothing separating these two players so far, in every category. Just gonna be a matter of who plays the big points better. Margins are razor thin.'

Emma's backhand crosscourt shot on the fourth rally stroke, sees Fernandez scrambling to hit a high ball, which falls wide. Fifteen thirty.

Emma hits a backhand crosscourt return winner off Fernandez's second serve. Two breakpoints and set points. Fifteen forty.

Mark Petchey: 'Astonishing! An outrageous bit of courage displayed there from Raducanu, coupled with extreme skill.'

Emma hits the fourth rally stroke a tiny fraction long. Still set point. She shrugs at her team, her body language saying, what more can I do? Thirty forty.

Emma's lob on the sixth rally stroke just goes long. Deuce.

Good return down the middle from Emma and Fernandez hits the next shot long. Set point again.

Second serve. Emma puts the return into the net. Second deuce.

The eighth rally stroke is a forehand crosscourt shot from Emma, deep into the corner. Fernandez hits high and wide. A fourth set point for Emma.

Emma pins Fernandez to her backhand corner then hits a forehand down the line winner. First set to Emma. Six-four.

***

Mark Petchey: 'Beautiful. Believe in fairy tales, children, because there's one happening right now in New York. Emma is a set away from winning the U.S. Open. Tim, wow! What can you say about that finish to the set?'

Tim Henman courtside: 'It's absolutely sensational. I cannot tell you, I mean it, for you to see it, for everyone to see the quality of the tennis point after point. They're just not taking a backward step. Raducanu is just looking to dictate, the quality of the ball striking is frightening. She's got the first set under her belt, but we should be under no illusion, Fernandez is not going anywhere. She is such a good competitor, she's got amazing support on her side, but what a start from Raducanu.'

Emma's talking to herself, nodding at what she's saying, playing the air conditioning over her face and neck, drinking the specially prepared pink drink and squeezing an energy bar from its wrapper. Fernandez is off court, so Emma's getting more time to recover.

Emma to serve.

Ace down the T. Fifteen love.

Emma puts the seventh rally stroke into the net. Fifteen all.

Emma keeps the next rally up the middle and Fernandez puts the twelfth rally stroke into the net. Thirty fifteen.

Fernandez skies the return. Forty fifteen.

A deep, wide serve and Emma runs in to hit a forehand winner behind the Canadian. One-love.

***

They change ends and Fernandez to serve.

Good return, and Fernandez hits the next shot wide. Love fifteen.

Double fault. Love thirty.

Fernandez hits the fifth rally stroke into the net off a shortish ground stroke from Emma. The unforced error brings three breakpoints. Love forty.

Emma rushes along the baseline to reach the fifth rally stroke, skies her shot and it lands long. Fernandez watched it all the way. Fifteen forty.

Good wide serve, Emma's forehand crosscourt return and Fernandez hits the backhand down the line winner. Second breakpoint saved. Just one left. Thirty forty.

Wonderful deep, wide serve from the leftie into Emma's backhand. Unreturnable. Deuce.

Emma's mishit return flies high and wide. Advantage Fernandez.

Another deep wide unreturnable serve. One game all.

Mark Petchey: 'That was a hugely significant hold of serve.'

***

Emma to serve.

An amazing display of close to the line shots. Fernandez misses out when the fifteenth rally stroke goes into the net. Fifteen love.

Emma hits the fifth rally stroke into the net, another unforced error. Fifteen all.

Brilliant crosscourt return from Fernandez sets the tone for the point. Emma puts the seventh rally stroke into the net. Fifteen thirty.

Martina Navratilova: 'Fernandez has picked up the pace here. Hitting the ball harder on both wings.'

Fernandez hits the top of the net on the eighth rally stroke, and it drops over. Emma can't quite get to it. Danger. Two breakpoints for the Canadian. Fifteen forty.

Martina Navratilova: 'The crowd is certainly getting behind Leylah Fernandez.'

The umpire calls for quiet.

Emma hits an unreturnable forehand down the line on the third rally stroke. Fernandez's reply hits the net. Still a breakpoint. Thirty forty.

Emma breaks her serve routine to wait for quiet.

Good second serve from Emma and Fernandez mishits into the net. Deuce.

The umpire calls for quiet again.

Great serve and Fernandez's mishit doesn't cross the net. Advantage to the Brit.

Emma hits the fifth rally stroke into the net post. Deuce number two.

Martina Navratilova: 'It was there for the taking. Tough shot. Needed a little more height. Hard to find openings. Both players move so beautifully and have really high tennis IQ, so they know where to be. The opponent tending to serve, well balanced, quick off the mark. It's great to watch.'

Forehand crosscourt from Fernandez on the fourth rally stroke. Breakpoint again.

Emma hits the fifth rally stroke into the net and Fernandez has the break. One-two.

Mark Petchey: 'Couple of games that have changed the complexion of this final completely.'

Martina Navratilova: 'Emma needs to hit a reset button here, as both games she had game points in. Love forty on returning, lost the game again. Then she crawled her way back up, had a game point, lost the game again, so she could be up three love. Instead, she's going into the break two one down, so she has to really dig down here, forget about that, try to get more aggressive. I think she's allowing Fernandez to be the aggressor here a little too much.'

***

Fernandez, serving, hits the fifth rally stroke long. Love fifteen.

Emma's forehand down the line return is a winner. Love thirty.

Martina Navratilova: 'That's more like it. Stepped into that one.'

Emma's crosscourt return just out. Fifteen thirty.

Martina Navratilova: 'Both players serving better in this set.'

Good crosscourt winner from Fernandez on the fifth rally stroke. Thirty all.

Emma lobs the sixth shot of the rally. Fernandez waits for it to come down in the very corner of the court, sends a high ball down the line and Emma hits a backhand crosscourt winner onto the side-line. Breakback point. Thirty forty.

Martina Navratilova: 'She made it, well, she took it early, was a dangerous shot, but the right shot, but I thought she was a little too early on that. What a great defensive lob here to get back into the point and then again you see her, she's on the baseline lurking. That dropped inside the side-line, beautifully done, breakback point.'

Second serve and Emma's signature backhand crosscourt return leaves Fernandez stranded. Back on serve. Two games all.

***

Emma, serving, hits the seventh rally stroke into the net. Love fifteen.

Emma's powerful forehand down the line on the third rally stroke forces Fernandez to sky the shot and Emma watches it carefully until it falls just out. Fifteen all.

Fernandez plays a dropshot return, Emma reaches it and her shot lands on the baseline, forcing the error and Fernandez plays into the net. Thirty fifteen.

Good shot from Fernandez causes Emma to hit wide on the seventh rally stroke. Thirty all.

Really deep, wide serve. Fernandez hits wide. Forty thirty.

Wonderful serve down the T is unreturnable. Emma shakes her fist at her team and Andrew Richardson shakes his back at her. Three-two.

***

Fernandez to serve. She hits Emma's return into the corner causing the Brit to mishit. Fifteen love.

Backhand winner down the line on the fourth rally stroke for Emma. Fifteen all.

Mark Petchey: 'Wow! An eighty-three mile per hour backhand winner.'

This time, Emma hits the fourth rally stroke for a forehand winner down the line. Fifteen thirty.

A poor return from Emma, but Fernandez overhits her crosscourt shot and it flies long. Two breakpoints. Fifteen forty.

The umpire calls for quiet between Fernandez's first and second serves.

Emma's return flies a fraction wide. Still breakpoint. Thirty forty.

On the third rally stroke, Emma hits an incredible forehand down the line to secure the break of serve. Four games to two.

Martina Navratilova: 'Oh, my God, what a guess, what a shot! That's the best shot of the tournament.'

Mark Petchey: 'Lightning reflexes. Is that the dagger? Is that the moment, is that the visual that will stay with us? A moment that felt like a painting.'

Martina Navratilova: 'The point of the match so far and she hits the best shot that I've seen her hit in this tournament, on that point now. This is a tough one to come back from for Leylah Fernandez.'

**

Emma to serve to try to consolidate the break. Ace wide and deep from Emma. Fifteen love.

Great rally. Fernandez getting the winner on the sixth rally stroke. Fifteen all.

Sixth rally stroke wide from Fernandez. Thirty fifteen.

A forehand crosscourt shot from Emma causes Fernandez to hit the fourth rally stroke into the net. Forty fifteen.

The umpire is calling for quiet and thanking the crowd—who are not keeping quiet. Emma waits patiently to serve, looking up into the terraces. Over twenty thousand stare back at her.

Emma's first serve is out. She shuffles wider along the baseline and delivers a deep, wide serve, which Fernandez returns long. Game to Emma. She's consolidated the break. 'Come on!' she screams, and her team shakes their fists and applaud. Five-two.

**

Martina Navratilova: 'She's been hugging that air conditioning all tournament long. Feeling the heat now, but in a good way. One game from following in Virginia Wade's footsteps.'

Fernandez serving to save the championship.

She hits the fifth rally stroke long. Love fifteen.

Emma hits the eighth rally stroke wide. Fifteen all.

Emma's return hits the net and she jumps up and down in annoyance at herself. Thirty fifteen.

Emma hits a defensive lob on the sixth rally stroke, which lands on the line in the corner. Fernandez replies, but it's high and in the middle of the court. Emma rushes in and hits a volley into Fernandez's forehand side, the Canadian returns it, high again, Emma smashes an overhead volley straight at Fernandez and she hits it into the net. An incredible point that had the crowd cheering throughout. Thirty all.

Emma is smiling as she returns to the baseline.

Fernandez hits the net cord off Emma's return and this time it drops on her side. Championship point for Emma. Thirty forty.

Emma mishits the fourth rally stroke and the ball flies between the net and the umpire's chair. Deuce.

Leylah Fernandez gives a wry smile. Not yet!

Fernandez swings the play from side to side and Emma hits the eighth rally stroke into the net. Advantage to the Canadian.

Fernandez mishits a shot off Emma's return. Second deuce.

Fernandez hits the fifth rally stroke wide, outside the tramlines. Second championship point for Emma.

An uncharacteristic error from Emma, hitting the fourth rally stroke into the net. Nerves? Deuce number three.

A fantastic down the line forehand from Fernandez on the ninth rally stroke, gives her the advantage point.

Emma hits the net on the tenth rally stroke. The match goes on. Game to Fernandez. Five-three.

***

Emma is going to have to serve for the match. Can she keep the nerves under control?

The crowd is cheering, whistling, and shouting out the players' names. The umpire calls for quiet several times.

Emma waits patiently to serve. Finally, the crowd realises that there'll be no play until the noise subsides.

Fernandez hits a forehand down the line winner on the sixth rally stroke. Love fifteen.

Martina Navratilova: 'She's definitely not lying down here. Raducanu's going to have to earn it.'

Fernandez's crosscourt, trying for a little too much, on the eighth rally stroke goes wide. Fifteen all.

A deep wide serve opens the court for Emma to fire a forehand winner down the line. Thirty fifteen.

Emma volleys into the net on the seventh rally stroke. Thirty all.

Great rally and Emma hits a lob on the ninth rally stroke. It lands long, watched by Fernandez all the way. Break point for the Canadian. During the point, on the seventh stroke of the rally, Emma slides to the shot and blood is running from her leg where it scraped along the court. Emma bends to look at the damage at the end of the point. Thirty forty.

She doesn't know what to do and looks towards the umpire's chair. Blood cannot be allowed to flow freely during a game and the umpire calls Emma to her seat. A trainer rushes onto the scene. Thirty forty, five two, the final of the U.S. Open, could there ever be a more dramatic moment, as if this match needed any more excitement. The commentators watch the replay.

Martina Navratilova: 'Where's that blood coming from. Oh, wow! That slide. Ouch! She needs a trainer to tape it up. They have to stop the match when a player's bleeding.'

Emma's sitting calmly while she's being treated. Fernandez is complaining to the referee, but it is not Emma's fault, and the umpire had no option. Understandable that Fernandez is upset, though. Breakpoint, with the momentum in a must-win game. Fernandez is now in tears over the

155

delay. The trainer is spraying the wound and Emma is wincing with the stinging pain.

Mark Petchey: 'Well, we needed to throw a little more drama on this, didn't we?'

There is enough blood showing through the dressing to show it is still bleeding profusely.

Emma leaves her seat and returns to the baseline to serve at thirty forty in the most important game of her life.

Fernandez's return catches Emma unawares and the rally begins. On the eighth rally stroke, Fernandez hits long. We're at deuce.

On the third rally stroke, Emma hits down the line. Fernandez seemingly had no way to get to it, but she did. Her lob lands in Emma's backhand corner. Emma's shot finds the baseline. Fernandez hits down the middle and Emma's forehand goes into Fernandez's backhand corner. They both fire crosscourt shots and then Emma hits long. The crowd explodes with cheers and applause. Breakpoint two for Fernandez.

Good serve, return to Emma's forehand, she hits down the line, Fernandez just gets to it and puts a loopy shot over the net. Emma runs in and hits a forehand volley at the Canadian. Fernandez tries to lob Emma, but it isn't high enough and the Brit plays an overhead volley, which Fernandez cannot get to. It's the second deuce.

Martina Navratilova: 'Fantastic stuff! Oh, my goodness, what an athlete, what a lob, under pressure, uncomfortable shot here, great forehand to get this short ball, Raducanu. Fernandez stays put, but this is an awkward overhead, what a great reach, she jumps so high on her serve. She had to do all the vertical on that one. Beautifully done.'

Fernandez skies the fourth rally shot. It's championship point again, for the third time.

Emma runs to her towel and walks back to the baseline and calmly begins her service routine.

An ace deep and wide and Emma collapses onto the court, her racquet thrown aside, and she rolls onto her back.

Emma has won the set, match and championship, six four, six three.

***

Mark Petchey: 'All hail, the queen of Queens. Emma Raducanu is the U.S. Open champion and what a way to do it.'

She scrambles to her feet, smiling, grinning, laughing. Her team are jumping for joy and hugging each other.

She hugs Leylah Fernandez and turns to look at the crowd, laughing, smiling, applauding them back and waving. Fernandez returns to her seat, fighting to hold back tears and hide her emotions.

Mark Petchey: 'And she does it, Martina, without dropping a set in the entire tournament, coming through from qualifying to the final.'

She wants to get to her team's box. Accompanied by two beefy security guards, she's ushered through a tunnel, upstairs and to the box. It seemingly takes an age to get to the team box and everyone is touching her, patting her and high fiving her on the way. Finally, she's there. A huge hug for Andrew Richardson, her coach, Will Herbert, the physio, Chris Helliar, her agent.

The security guards lead her back from the box and down to the court again, everyone she passes wanting to pat her shoulders and arms.

Catherine Whitaker in the studio: 'What just happened? Emma Raducanu is a Grand Slam champion. Take nothing from this young woman that was sitting her A-levels in Bromley three months ago. She is about to collect the U.S. Open trophy from Billie Jean King. It's beyond what any of us could have ever imagined. Tim Henman watched it all from courtside.'

Tim Henman: 'It's an absolute joke, Catherine. I'm shaking, my legs are like jelly. I cannot believe the resilience, how tough she was, the quality of tennis, but these great champions, they find a way to get it done. In a context, in the history of our sport, she was in qualifying three weeks ago, she won ten matches without dropping a set. It's an

157

absolute joke. Both girls executed such a high level. I really want to mention Fernandez, as well, coz she's an unbelievable competitor. She's got a huge future, but on the day, Raducanu was too good.'

Catherine Whitaker: 'Tim, you were the very first person she looked at when she won the title there.'

The PA system begins to play *Sweet Caroline* and Emma is laughing, clapping and singing along with it from her seat. Union flags are being waved from various locations around the ground as the teenager tries to take in, to absorb the adoration, perhaps trying to come to terms with the enormity of what she's accomplished.

The two players step up onto the hastily constructed stage and take their places either side of Mary Joe Fernandez.

Mary Joe Fernandez raises the microphone: 'Ladies and gentlemen, how about another round of applause for a terrific final and for Emma and Leylah.'

Emma is full of smiles, but Leylah is having trouble forcing a loser's smile. The Canadian is clearly distressed. So near, yet so far. As they stand on the platform, blood is, once again, seeping from the dressing on Emma's leg.

Mary Joe Fernandez speaking over the crowd noise as Leylah steps forward: 'They love you, Leylah. It was an incredible tournament; I know you're disappointed but what do you think of everything that you've accomplished these last two weeks.'

Leylah Fernandez: 'It's so incredible. I have no idea what to say today. It's gonna be hard to recuperate, but Emma played amazing, so congratulations to Emma and to your team, but you know what, I'm very proud of myself with the way I played these past two weeks, and especially having the crowd packed in New York has been amazing. It's definitely special for me to be here in a final. Thanks for having you cheering me on, thank you so much, New York, thank you everyone.'

Mary Joe Fernandez: 'And now it's time for our champion, Emma Raducanu. Emma, the crowd loves you too. You started this journey three weeks ago, you're the first qualifier to ever win a major tournament. How did you do it?'

Emma Raducanu: 'First of all, I really want to congratulate Leylah and her team on an incredible fortnight. I mean, she's played some incredible tennis and beaten some of the top players in the world, so it was an incredibly difficult match, but I thought the level was extremely high and I hope that we play each other in many more tournaments, and hopefully finals.' She looks around at Fernandez and they both smile. 'As for the three weeks I've spent in New York, I would say that having such a supportive team like I have over there, my coach, Will, the LTA, my agent, everyone in that team, and everyone back home who isn't here but watching on TV, thank you so much for all your support over the years, and most of all, I would say thank you to everyone here in New York. Thank you all for making me feel so at home from my first qualifying match, all the way to the final. I've loved playing in front of you and you've really spurred me on in some very difficult moments and I hope that me and Leylah put on a good performance today.'

Mary Joe Fernandez: 'And, finally, speaking of another legend, Virginia Wade has been watching all your matches. She's here to witness, she's the last one to win a major from Great Britain. What does that mean to you?'

Emma: 'It means so much to have Virginia here, and also Tim. To have such British legends and icons for me to follow in their footsteps helps, and definitely gave me the belief that I could actually do it.'

Mary Joe Fernandez: 'Congratulations, Emma. And now to hand you the prize money cheque, are you ready for how much? *Two point five **million** dollars*, is Andrea Lisher, head of JP Morgan Asset Management.'

Emma takes the envelope, which is immediately whisked away by a tournament official. Emma says something to Leylah about it, and whatever it was, it brings a smile to the runner-up's stoic face.

Mary Joe Fernandez: 'And now, Emma, the great Billie Jean King will present you with the champion trophy.'

Bille Jean, dressed in blue jacket and black trousers, picks up the heavy cup and passes it to Emma, both examining the silverware and looking at the engraved names of the previous champions. A few inaudible words pass between them.

Mary Joe Fernandez: 'Ladies and gentlemen, the 2021 U.S. Open Women's Champion – Emma Raducanu!'

Emma smiles, looks around the stadium and is surprised by red, white, and blue streamers falling from somewhere above and littering the stage.

Catherine Whitaker in the studio: 'It is so hard for us to take this all in, so goodness knows how eighteen year old Emma Raducanu is taking it all in. It does look like she's doing just that. She's gazing around this Arthur Ashe Stadium, gazing lovingly at the trophy, Billie Jean King standing behind her, beaming broadly at her, and of course, Leylah Fernandez as well. Find someone that looks at you the way Virginia Wade looks at Emma Raducanu. Annie, what are we watching here?'

Anne Keothavong in the studio: 'It still feels so surreal, I mean that was just an incredible performance from Emma and from Leylah, a really high-quality tennis match from two teenagers, but honestly, I never thought I'd see a British female lift a Grand Slam trophy in my lifetime, and I just can't put it into words how huge this is. This is, perhaps, one of the greatest sporting achievements *ever*, I just, I don't know, I want to say I'm just so happy for her and the way she started. To not drop a set throughout this tournament, I mean, this just isn't normal, this doesn't happen, it's unheard of. This is just an unbelievable achievement.'

A kneeling squad of some thirty photographers are taking hundreds of rapid-fire photographs of the two women with their trophies.

Now the cameras are flashing just at Emma, as she holds the trophy high above her head, beaming her winning smile, bemused at the adoration. She kisses it for the images and hugs it to her chest with her eyes shut as we show on the book cover.

Catherine Whitaker: Let's hear from Emma Raducanu with her personal cheerleader, Tim Henman.'

Tim Henman courtside with the champion and her silverware: 'Emma, many congratulations. You've been in New York for three weeks, qualified, and you just became U.S. Open champion. Can you put that into words?'

Emma, still hugging the trophy: 'Not at all. Honestly, I'm still so shocked, still in the moment, I can't believe I came through that last service game. It honestly means absolutely everything to just hold this trophy, and yeah, I just don't wanna let go right now.'

Tim Henman: 'Talk to me about the start of the match, your tension, nervousness coming in. How did you feel at the beginning?'

Emma: 'Yeah, honestly, yesterday and this morning there was a bit of like weird feelings that I couldn't quite put my finger on. I didn't know what it was, but I think that's just normal, and when I came out on court I felt completely at home, I felt completely like business as usual, I was just focusing one point in a time. I think the level was extremely high, both of us playing some unbelievable tennis, and yeah, I had to fight really hard to just cling onto that first set and then keep my nose in front in the second.'

Tim Henman: 'And what did you feel were the key areas for you to be able to dominate your game style against Fernandez?'

Emma: 'I think it was implementing my serve and return. I don't think I served as best as I have been throughout the tournament, but honestly in the key moments it definitely helped, and I came up with some clutch serves when I needed them. And I think changing direction as early as possible because if you gave it to her a couple more times, she would change on you and you were running and she's extremely good at that.'

Tim Henman: 'Many congratulations. Enjoy the party tonight.'

Emma: 'Thank you very much.'

And she turns away for another interview, with several more TV crews patiently waiting in line.

Greg Rusedski in the studio: 'This is like a dream come true. This we will never see again in men's or women's tennis, a qualifier and somebody to win ten matches at a slam, without losing a set. I mean it is truly a fairy tale.'

Raducanu's Fairy Tale in New York is now complete.

Bibiane Schoofs	6-1; 6-2.
Mariam Bolkvadze	6-3; 7-5.
Mayar Sherif	6-1; 6-4.
Stefanie Vögele	6-2; 6-3.
Shuai Zhang	6-2; 6-4.
Sara Sorribes Tormo	6-0; 6-1.
Shelby Rogers	6-2; 6-1.
Belinda Bencic	6-3; 6-4.
Maria Sakkari	6-1; 6-4.
Leylah Fernandez	6-4; 6-3.

One hundred and twenty games won and only fifty lost in ten incredible matches, without losing a set.

Postscript

Following the Fairy Tale in New York, Emma became brand ambassador for Tiffany & Co., Dior, Evian, British Airways, Vodafone, and Porsche. She was appointed Member of the Order of the British Empire in the New Year's Honours for services to tennis. She went on to win Britain's Sports Personality of the Year, WTA Newcomer of the Year, and Sunday Times Sportswoman of the Year.

Since that heady day on 11th September 2021, Martina Navratilova's words during the Bencic game have never been more incisive, 'She's just a superstar in the making. You don't want to put too much pressure on anybody, but you know when they're special. The only really biggest concern is health. If the body is willing, I think everything else is there.'

Since the U.S. Open, Emma has not had the best of results. She caught Covid while preparing for the Australian Open. This meant that she didn't handle a racquet for three weeks. Out of condition from the setback, she lost games, developed blisters trying to recover fitness, then a bad hip or back developed and it took her until Roland Garros, the French Open to become injury free, and that was only temporary. A side strain at Nottingham on grass, saw her retire after just a few games. It seemed to occur on the first or second serve of the match. She tried to continue but was unable to do so.

Although she claims to like clay courts, they were a steep learning curve, and frankly, the slow way that the red courts play does not seem to suit Emma's powerful style. Nevertheless, Emma met world number one, Iga Swaitek in the quarterfinals of the Porsche Tennis Grand Prix and was beaten 6-4, 6-4. It was a creditable performance on an unfamiliar surface, and in the second set, Emma managed to break Swaitek's serve. This fan would love to see a rematch when Emma is fully fit.

As this book goes to press, we were expecting to see her play at Eastbourne, but she did not apply for a wildcard. Her advisers wanted her to have longer to recover. Next, of course, is Wimbledon, where the fairy tale really began. This fan, with many tens of thousands of others, has his fingers crossed, but expectations should not be too high. Her lawn tennis preparation has only been a handful of games. She says, herself, that her body is still developing to cope with the physical pressure of the WTA tour and that she needs time to get things right.

She is receiving great support from the LTA and there have been words of encouragement from the likes of Andy Murray, Paula Badosa, and one of the players she defeated during the Fairy Tale, Maria Sakkari.

She is still in her first full year of the WTA tour and expecting her to win every tournament she enters is unrealistic. What she needs is time to improve fitness and get used to the rigors of playing twenty or more tournaments per year.

Whatever the future holds, no one can ever take away her achievement at Flushing Meadows, New York in 2021.

Tony's Other Books

Thank you for reading *RADUCANU'S FAIRY TALE IN NEW YORK*.

Primarily, I am a science fiction author, but not the shoot-em-up or *Star Wars* variety. My stories tend to be on the realistic end of the scale, asking 'what if' questions in a modern world that we all recognise.

FEDERATION – what if a benevolent galactic empire of a quarter of a million worlds stumbled across Earth and asked if we wanted to join? Our first problem would be understanding that individual nations are no longer feasible and, when the newcomers offer us robots capable of carrying out every conceivable task, better, more efficiently, quicker and more accurately than humans. There is no longer any need to work for a living, but is the result some sort of communist utopia? Federation is the first of a trilogy dealing with Earth's reaction.

MINDSLIP – what if a cosmic event affected every mind on Earth. Not just people, but animals and even insects, molluscs and fish? Astrophysicist, Geoff Arnold, is the protagonist. He wakes up in a strange body and discovers his family have vanished into a world he can hardly recognise. Join him to find out how the situation resolves itself into a new improbable reality.

THE VISITOR – what if the first space junk elimination expedition discovers a small, ancient, badly damaged artefact in low Earth orbit. Dynamic female astronaut, Evelyn Slater, finds herself emersed in the politics of government secrecy as the world fails to come to terms with the fact that we might not be alone in the universe after all.

MOONSCAPE – what if astronauts at the first proper moonbase find something in the moon dust? Something which has been hibernating for millennia, something parasitic, which has the objective of total domination of other living creatures. This story is the first of five adventures of Mark Noble. The parasite is not what it was first thought to be, and each story leads on from that first encounter into books which deal with humankind's early exploratory journeys to the stars.

THE DOOR – what if aliens have occupied a disused convent in a sleepy English seaside town? One man and his dog find evidence. It leads into an adventure to save the human race from disaster, but not as you might expect.

Other non-fiction by Tony Harmsworth:

SCOTLAND'S BLOODY HISTORY – the complex and convoluted history of the world's oldest kingdom, particularly in relation to its southern neighbour. If you've never quite understood the relationship of the two nations – this book simplifies it from the Scottish perspective.

LOCH NESS, NESSIE and ME – the most comprehensive book ever written about the famous mystery, by a local resident who has been involved in many of the most important expeditions. Discover the truth.

Links to find all of these books are on the author's website, Harmsworth.net.

Reader Club

Building a relationship with my readers is the very best thing about being a writer. In these days of the internet and email, the opportunities to interact with you is unprecedented. I send occasional newsletters which include special offers and information on how the various series are developing. You can keep in touch by signing up for my no-spam mailing list.

Sign up at my webpage: https://harmsworth.net or on my **TonyHarmsworthAuthor** Facebook page and you will know when my books are released and will get free material from time to time and other information.

If you have questions, don't hesitate to write to me at Tony@Harmsworth.net.

FREE BOOK

If you would like to try one of my science fiction novels free of charge, just join the free Reader Club on the following link and download MOONSCAPE FREE.

References

[i] Female Genital Mutilation

[ii] For the first time, the 2021 US Open championship has the automatic Hawkeye line-call system on all courts.

[iii] From Amazon Prime coverage, August 25th, 2021.

[iv] From Amazon Prime coverage, August 26th, 2021. Dave Leno and Jesse Levine.

[v] From Amazon Prime coverage, August 27th, 2021. Dave Leno and Jesse Levine.

[vi] From US Open Prime coverage pre-match interview with Mark Petchey, August 30th, 2021.

[vii] Women's Tennis Association.

[viii] From US Open Prime coverage, 30th August 2021. Catherine Whitaker, Daniella Hantuchova and Annabel Croft in the studio and Tim Henman, Sam Smith, Karthi Gnanasegaram and Anne Keothavong courtside.

[ix] Nigel Sears, Andy Murray's father in law, was Emma's coach during Wimbledon 2021 and before.

[x] From US Open Prime coverage, 2nd September 2021. Anne Keothavong, Sam Smith, Tim Henman, Annabel Croft and Greg Rusedski

[xi] From US Open Prime coverage, 4th September 2021. Catherine Whitaker, Karthi Gnanasegaram, Tim Henman, Sam Smith, Anne Keothavong, Annabel Croft and Greg Rusedski.

[xii] The Fed Cup is the Billie Jean King Cup, the World Team Cup of Women's Tennis.

[xiii] Iga Swaitek became world number one when Ash Barty retired and, at the time of writing this book, she has won thirty-four consecutive matches and looks invincible.

[xiv] From US Open Prime coverage, 6th September 2021. Catherine Whitaker, Greg Rusedski, Mark Petchey, Martina Navratilova, Rennae Stubbs and Tim Henman.

[xv] The 2020 Olympics were postponed to 2021 owing to the pandemic.

[xvi] From US Open Prime coverage, 8th September 2021. Catherine Whitaker, Annabel Croft, Greg Rusedski, Mark Petchey, Mary Joe

Fernandez, Anne Keothavong, Rennae Stubbs, Jim Courier and Tim Henman.

[xvii] From US Open Prime coverage, 10th September 2021. Marcus Buckland, Greg Rusedski, Annabel Croft, Mark Petchey, Martina Navratilova, Rennae Stubbs and Tim Henman.

[xviii] Race rankings are for the calendar year, from 1st January, while the world rankings take a full twelve months. If you lose early in a tournament you did well in the previous year, last year's points are deducted and the current year's added. With race rankings, you start with zero and all your points accumulate until 31st December when, of course, they match the world ranking points.

[xix] Lawn Tennis Association.

[xx] From US Open Prime coverage, 11th September 2021. Greg Rusedski, Anne Keothavong, Mark Petchey, Martina Navratilova, Rennae Stubbs, Mary Joe Fernandez, Catherine Whitaker and Tim Henman.

Printed in Great Britain
by Amazon

10321393R00098